C000066869

Monty Panesar

The Full Monty

Monty Panesar
The Full Monty

Monty Panesar

with

Fred Atkins

WHITE OWL
AN IMPRINT OF PEN & SWORD BOOKS LTD.
YORKSHIRE – PHILADELPHIA

First published in Great Britain in 2019 by
Pen & Sword White Owl
An imprint of
Pen & Sword Books Ltd
Yorkshire - Philadelphia

ISBN 978 1 52675 450 9

A CIP catalogue record for this book is available from the British Library.

Typeset in INDIA by IMPEC eSolutions
Printed and bound in the UK by TJ International

Pen & Sword Books Ltd incorporates the Imprints of Pen & Sword
Books Archaeology, Atlas, Aviation, Battleground, Discovery,
Family History, History, Maritime, Military, Naval, Politics, Railways,
Select, Transport, True Crime, Fiction, Frontline Books, Leo Cooper,
Praetorian Press, Seaforth Publishing, Wharncliffe and White Owl.

For a complete list of Pen & Sword titles please contact

PEN & SWORD BOOKS LIMITED
47 Church Street, Barnsley, South Yorkshire, S70 2AS, England
E-mail: enquiries@pen-and-sword.co.uk
Website: www.pen-and-sword.co.uk

or

PEN AND SWORD BOOKS
1950 Lawrence Rd, Havertown, PA 19083, USA
E-mail: uspen-and-sword@casematepublishers.com
Website: www.penandswordbooks.com

Contents

Foreword

Characters in sport are hard to come by these days, but it's fair to say that Monty Panesar is one of them. He was a dressing room and crowd favourite, not just because of his skills as a slow, left-arm bowler, but also because of his exuberance and love, both for the game and for life in general.

I had the pleasure of captaining Monty in his first Test in India and will never forget him taking the wicket of the great Sachin Tendulkar, his first in international cricket. Nor will I forget his celebrations afterwards!

He did cause me a few headaches, mainly when I was trying to position him in the field. It wasn't just a question of deciding where the ball wouldn't go: we also had to take into account his ability to wander 40 yards from where he was actually placed.

I'll never forget him dropping MS Dhoni in Mumbai when he was at long off and then, in the next over, taking a far harder catch in the same position effectively to win the match. This to me sums up Monty both as a player and a person. He's a winner, someone who'll never shy away from a challenge, no matter how far outside his comfort zone he may be.

He has a steely determination which is hidden by a softer, friendlier exterior, as the Aussies found out in Cardiff in 2009.

This, to me, was Monty's finest hour. Against all the odds, against an Aussie team sniffing victory, out strode the great man, playing every shot he'd practised in the nets on the long walk to the middle. Ponting and his boys must have thought going 1-0 up was a certainty with 40 minutes still left to take the final wicket.

I'm not going to lie. Sat on the balcony with the lads, we'd resigned ourselves to our impending doom.

Not Monty.

To this day I believe he saw this as an opportunity to show off the hours of batting practice he'd put in, but more importantly, he saw it as a chance to show the world that under the most extreme pressure, with the odds against him, he would prevail. And of course he did!

Ponting and his men were left moaning and whingeing about time wasting, while our hero and Jimmy Anderson were left to take the plaudits. The smile on his face as he came off is one I'll never forget.

Since those days I know Monty has had to overcome more difficult odds in his life outside cricket, but with his steady determination, winner's mentality and that smile that I'll never get tired of seeing, no challenge is too great.

Thank you again for all your efforts on the cricket field and also for the chats in the dressing room and in bars about life and your faith; they made me think about how I live my own life and how I can try to be a better person.

Like the rest of the cricketing world, I have your back, always. And to anyone who has a problem with Monty, I can assure you it's not him, it's you!

Your mate,
Fred

Introduction

This is the story of an all-consuming ambition, of a glimpse of greatness preceding a descent into the dark, of paranoia, of fractured relationships, frayed friendships and one broken marriage.

It's a story of racism and overcoming it: the extreme form faced by my parents' generation, the dog-whistle variety typified by Norman Tebbit's 'cricket test' and the unconscious bias that still affects British Asian cricketers.

It becomes story of hope, faith in humanity and ultimately, redemption, both personal and collective.

It was the integration of white English and immigrant Sikh communities that made it possible for a wide-eyed boy from Luton to briefly achieve his goal of becoming the best spin bowler in the world.

It was the love of my family, my fellow Sikhs and the cricket community that helped me to heal when the pressure I put on myself to regain that status almost crippled me with paranoia.

I think it would make a great biopic. Martin Scorsese could be the director and a handsome, young Bollywood actor would play the younger version of me before I take over the title role, as both the villain and the hero.

In the climactic final scenes I'd tumble, like Alan Rickman falling backwards off a skyscraper in *Die Hard*, only to rise again like Christian Bale in *Batman*, emerging from the pit.

I wanted to write a feel-good book and I hope you find it uplifting to read. I want to send out a message of love, positivity and aspiration, because although it wasn't the life I expected to lead and things didn't always go to plan, in the great stories they never do.

Monty Panesar
Luton, 2019

'Like a Stunned Halibut'

I wanted to be famous for my cricketing prowess. In my daydreams I imagined playing in about 150 Test matches, beating Murali's record of 800 Test wickets and conjuring a ball of the millennium that would make Shane Warne's so-called 'ball of the century' look like a rank long hop. I wanted to be The Greatest Spin Bowler in the World, but also, like Warney, I wanted to be respected for my specialist fielding skills and my match-turning batting cameos down the order.

As the first Sikh to play for England, as well as The Greatest Spin Bowler in the World, I'd be knighted, and after the Queen had said 'Arise Sir Monty,' I'd retire to the Buckingham Palace gardens, where Prince Philip and I would share a glass of champagne and I'd laugh at his risky jokes about my patka.

At some point in my forties, with a couple of World Cup winners' medals hanging around my neck, I'd retire as a revered elder statesman of the game and move seamlessly into the commentary box, where Aggers would offer me a slice of Victoria sponge sent from a listener in Wittersham, Geoffrey Boycott would ask me how many Test match centuries I'd scored and I'd get revenge on Henry Blofeld for calling me Monty Python by 'accidentally' calling him Ernst Stavro.

It didn't quite happen that way. My career took an unexpected trajectory, partly because of a ball that took an unexpected trajectory from MS Dhoni's bat in 2006, during the third and final Test in Mumbai.

At least sixteen catches went down in the match, but the one that sealed my reputation came in India's second innings, when India were 90-6, needing another 223 to win. More realistically, they needed to bat out the final session for the draw and blocking wasn't really Dhoni's forte. He was the sort of player who didn't really think a shot was worth six runs unless he'd hit it into the upper tier of the stand and I'd already dropped him once in the first innings when he'd driven a ball that thudded into my chest.

Now it looked as though he was planning to monster Shaun Udal. Dhoni shaped to hit a six but instead hit Udal's delivery almost vertically into the sun. I thought I had it, and then it just disappeared for what seemed like a year but was probably only a couple of seconds.

I panicked. The sun was so bright it was literally blinding, but I knew I had to do something. I calculated the odds. If I stood there, unable to see a thing but with my hands in an orthodox catching position, the chances of reeling the ball in successfully were somewhere in the region of one in a million. The alternative was to stand there, still unable to see a thing, but without my hands in an orthodox catching position. If I did that, the chances of success were precisely zero.

It wasn't much of a choice, but the first option was clearly better than the latter, so I held my hands out. It was then that I heard a thud and saw the ball land 2 metres to the right of me. You couldn't even call it a drop because I hadn't got anywhere near it. It was probably the funniest thing you've ever seen on a cricket field, if you were anyone but me. Or Shaun Udal. He wasn't angry; he just stood there with his mouth gaping open like a stunned halibut. The other person who failed to see the funny side was our coach, Duncan Fletcher. Duncan was good at failing to see the funny side of things.

My other teammates were laughing. I'd always liked making people laugh, but this wasn't what I'd had in mind. 'I wouldn't worry about it, mate,' said absolutely no one.

As part of our media training, the ECB had given us a card stating the team's core values. Always be upbeat. Don't be political. Back your teammates. Never criticise the opposition. Nowhere on the card did it provide instructions for how to react when you'd made the worst fielding error of all time in front of an audience of tens of millions.

What could I do? Style it out like Del Boy, picking himself up and fixing his tie after falling through an open bar? I already knew this was going to be shown on a compilation of cricket's biggest blunders. I didn't realise I'd end up presenting the video.

This, perhaps, was the moment I became 'Monty, the cult hero'. I was happy with the hero bit, but I'm still not sure about the 'cult' part. I wanted to be The Greatest Spin Bowler in the World and for that to happen I needed to be mentioned in the same company as Shane Warne and Murali. Instead I became Monty Panesar: The Brand.

Three balls after The Miss of the Century, I caught Dhoni, in an almost identical position, to an almost identical shot.

By then, however, I could already see a vision of my future as the Sikh Phil Tufnell. Like Tuffers, I had a good career. Like Tuffers, I've been on television shows like *Celebrity MasterChef* and *Dancing on Ice*. Like Tuffers, I've had to endure a degree of tabloid infamy.

There are things that I've done that I'm not proud of and I've suffered serious mental health issues. Mental illness stalked my generation of English cricketers. One by one I watched it pick off my teammates. When Marcus Trescothick first admitted he'd been suffering from depression in 2008 I was shocked, but I didn't think anything like that would ever happen to me. In the wake of his revelations, the PCA provided its members with a booklet telling us what to do if we experienced anything similar. I threw my copy in the bin.

I subsequently began to struggle with a different condition: paranoia. It affected my personality to the extent that it also seriously affected both my physical health and my relationships with my family and teammates.

By writing this book I want to highlight these issues, but I also want to stress that not only can you survive them; you can also overcome them and go on to live a full and enjoyable life again.

It's now twelve years since the Mumbai Test. At the time of writing, four years have elapsed since I last played for England and yet, I'm still probably one of the most recognisable cricketers in the country. Some of this is down to the way I look: in a showroom full of red cars, a lilac car is going to stand out.

But it's also because, like Tuffers, people still seem to love me. I thought the adoration would have died down after I stopped playing for England, but it's exactly the same. Part of the reason people feel they can identify with me is because I'm human. I'd make mistakes in the field, but they'd forgive me.

Maybe it's easier to relate to someone who's flawed than someone like Kevin Pietersen, who's nearly as handsome as I am and is built like a Greco-South African god: 6' 4" tall and with barely an ounce of fat on him. He's also an authentic genius, and there's no point being a genius if you're going to hide your talent. When he unveiled the switch hit for the first time, all that the bowler Scott Styris could do was shrug and smile. It was a brilliant piece of cricket, but it wasn't something the average person could emulate.

Stuart Broad is another player who's so good-looking that if we walked into a room together, some of the women might be forgiven for looking at him rather than me. He's 6' 5", with blue eyes and beautiful blond hair that magically seemed to stop receding when he was in his early twenties.

He's been a phenomenal player for England throughout his career. There might be only one or two people in a billion who are capable of taking 8-15 in a Test match with Australia. For that reason, it's maybe less easy to identify with him than it is with someone who cremates a salmon on a reality cookery show. Whatever the reason for all this love, the feeling is mutual.

Would I have achieved this level of fame and popularity if I'd caught Dhoni first time? Probably not.

But I still wish I'd fucking caught it ...

Chapter 1

Most Popular Dog Names of 2006

Bliss it was that dawn to be alive, but to be in Luton was very heaven.

William Wordsworth

This conversation has happened to me more than once.

'Are you Monty Panesar?'

'Yes.'

'Mate, I named my dog after you!'

If the question 'What was the most popular dog's name of 2006?' ever crops up on *Who Wants To Be A Millionaire*, you can bet your mortgage it'll be 'Monty'.

It's a great English name and there's so much history behind it. For a lot of people, the first person they'll think of when they hear the word 'Monty' is Field Marshall Bernard Montgomery, an authentic British hero of the Second World War and a man who'll be revered well after I and everyone reading this book has gone.

There's the TV gardener Monty Don, the film *The Full Monty*, the character Uncle Monty from the cult film *Withnail & I*, and then there's Monty Python, the name by which an apparently confused Henry Blofeld once referred to me during a commentary, to general hilarity. It didn't take a lot to confuse Henry, as I'd later find out.

Well-meaning, white English people would struggle to pronounce Mudhsuden (try Mud-Huh-Syoo-Den) and by the time my teenage years were out I was universally known as Monty.

Many Sikhs in England now have English names and I think that's great because it shows we're integrating into society. It also makes life a lot easier when you're in the changing room. When people asked me my name I'd say Mudhsuden, and they'd immediately ask if I had a nickname. I'd reply, 'Monty' and they'd say, 'Great, we'll call you that.' It helps when you're socialising because it's a lot easier for English people to say and a lot of my relatives think it's a great name.

When I was picked for England it was a big deal for the Sikh community, a big deal for the Punjabi community and a big deal for the 3 million South Asians living in the UK. They needed someone to look up to, like a role model, to say, 'You know what? Things can happen, barriers can be broken, not just in sport but in business and everywhere in society.'

People started to change their style, copying the way I wore my headgear, tied at the back and then a pony tail. British Asians at the very top of their professions have told me how much it means to them to see a man in a turban bowling for his country, and the ECB were proud that there was a Sikh playing for England. I think they thought it was great for our country, not just for cricket. It was like a way of celebrating how cosmopolitan and multi-cultural society was in England and how far ahead it was of other nations. At the time, however, I didn't fully appreciate the impact my selection would have. Nor did I realise quite how far we'd come.

***

I was born Mudhsuden Singh Panesar, to Paramajit Singh and Gursharan Kaur, on Sunday, 25 April 1982, in Luton, Bedfordshire. This was during the height of the Falklands Crisis, on the day that British troops recaptured the island of South Georgia. Therefore, in the Martin Scorsese-directed biopic of my life, this is where we cut between the maternity ward of Luton Hospital and footage of British troops raising the Union flag on a South Atlantic island. We cut to Prime Minister Margaret Thatcher telling the nation, 'Just rejoice at that news,' and go back to the maternity ward, where my mother hands me to my father for the first time.

As far as the soundtrack is concerned, I entered the world just as Paul McCartney and Stevie Wonder were top of the UK charts with a song called *Ebony and Ivory*, a tune with an unsubtle message about black people and white people living together in perfect harmony.

I had a healthy, happy childhood in Luton, which might come as a surprise to anyone's who's done an internet search on the town and seen it described as 'the worst place to live in the UK' by the *Daily Telegraph* in 2016.

It isn't. Luton's fine. Nearly a quarter of a million people live there and it's one of the most diverse towns in the country. I still live on the outskirts. We have had some extremism and the English Defence League was formed there, but the problems are exaggerated and our everyday lives aren't defined by the actions of a few idiots.

When I was selected to play for my country it was a source of real civic pride in Luton, maybe because it isn't a town with a rich track record for producing international sportsmen. Kerry Dixon, the Chelsea and England footballer, was born there, and Luton Town FC have produced a handful of England players like Paul Walsh, Ricky Hill and Brian Stein, but as far as I know, I wasn't just the first Sikh to play cricket for England … I was also the first Lutonian.

If you need any more evidence of integration, Luton now has second-generation immigrant taxi drivers who are fanatical Luton Town fans and speak with accents that are half-Punjabi and half-Bedfordshire. My own accent could probably be described as having a slightly posh, home counties, BBC style, but I do have a habit of saying 'Do you know what I mean?' at the end of sentences.

I'm also fluent in Punjabi and I can get by in a couple of other languages as well, including Hindi and a few words of French. I was once invited onto the pitch at The Emirates, as the half-time guest of honour, and managed to say '*J'adore Arsene Wenger*' to the 60,000 people in the stadium.

***

There's something about England and the UK that the world loves. I think it's something to do with etiquette, behaviour, structure and education. It's about human equality: if you're sick, the NHS will take care of you, no matter how wealthy or poor you are.

My family is originally from India, where there's a saying that if you have money, you have four friends, but if you have no money, you'll have none. It isn't like that in England and it all boils down to one point: it's a great place to be a human being.

Or at least, it is now.

Chapter 2

'Sorry We've Invaded Your Country'

Ebony and Ivory did not sing together in perfect harmony in Luton during the 1960s. My parents' generation were the victims of an extreme kind of racism when they arrived in the UK and the average Sikh did not finish his shift and walk into a working men's club to sit side by side at a piano with his white English colleagues.

Luton was only just getting used to the Irish when a wave of immigration from the sub-continent, which included first my uncle and then my parents, transformed the town. This was a direct legacy of the British Empire, about which I have ambivalent feelings. On the one hand, you could argue the British spent 300 years looting the sub-continent. On the other, I'm not sure I'd be here if they hadn't.

In his TV series *Empire*, Jeremy Paxman described it as a 'protection racket', and it was an astonishingly effective con trick. At one point, 6,000 British officials managed to control 200 million Indians. One governor said: 'If each black man were to take up a handful of sand and by united effort throw it upon the white-faced intruders, we should be buried alive.'

That never happened, because the British knew how to divide and rule. The local maharajah was allowed to keep his territory provided he paid the British a 'tribute', and an Indian ruling class was established. They began dressing and even speaking like their occupiers and about 75,000 of them would die serving Britain during the First World War. Another 87,000, including soldiers from the areas now known as Nepal, Bangladesh and Pakistan, died in the Second World War.

At this point the British decided to open the gates to anyone from what was now known as the Commonwealth who wanted to come to Britain for a better life. It seemed like quite a kind gesture, a way of saying 'Sorry we've invaded your country,' and it also had the less altruistic advantage of helping relieve the labour shortage caused by six years of war.

Unfortunately, some people didn't see it that way. They blocked out the bit where India had been plundered of its natural and human resources and just saw the hordes of people coming over here to invade their small island. To which I'd reply, 'Well then, the British Empire should not have invaded

India.' You can't go to a country as an invader, take all of their jewels, all their goods, and then go back to England and say, 'Right, now we're going to shut the gates because we've robbed all your stuff and we're not going to help your people.'

What's the relationship here? Sorry we've come to your country, nicked all your stuff, and then that's it? Why did the British Empire invade India in the first place, and why weren't they happy with what they had? The answer is: power. That's why. It's an interesting debate because one minute you think, 'They've nicked all our goods,' the next minute you think, 'Well actually, what has the British Empire given to India?' They gave India the railway system, which connects the whole of the country, and they gave the universal language of English, so it's not all about looting.

Yet even now, the quality of life in India is very basic. I think the average Indian earns £2,000–£3,000 per year. You can buy a meal for £1 and for one to two pounds per day you can actually feed yourself very well. You can buy a house there for thirty to fifty grand and actually live very comfortably, so one advantage of India is that the cost of living is low. Food and petrol are cheap, and property is not expensive unless you want to live in super-exclusive areas.

In Britain, however, there's more human value. We have to work really hard in this country because the cost of living is much higher, but people value human life and that's what makes England so special. If you go to India it's all about the money. Over there, if someone's dying or struggling, they can't afford the basic medical care and it's very difficult for the poor people, so you can understand why the idea of coming to England was so attractive.

***

My uncle moved first, in the 1960s. In 1977, my dad followed him and started working as a carpenter at the Vauxhall Motors plant. They both came because they, like a lot of people, thought they would have a better life in England than they could at home. My mum came here for a holiday and ended up staying after she'd met my dad.

It was this first generation that absorbed the full force of the racism. To put this into perspective, it wasn't anything like as bad as the abuse black or brown people were taking in South Africa or the USA at the same time. They didn't have to put up with segregation or people burning down their places of worship, but if they went into pubs they'd be told, 'Get out of here, you don't belong here,' or worse.

The insult of choice was 'Paki', regardless of whether they were from India, Pakistan, Bangladesh or Sri Lanka. The more direct abuse usually came from people who'd never seen brown or black faces before – white men and women who'd grown up in Luton and had never been anywhere else – but it wasn't exclusively uneducated people who were the problem. Middle and upper-class families wouldn't necessarily say anything to an Asian's face but they were happy to use the P-word behind their backs and to laugh at comedians with racist acts, like Bernard Manning. Shopkeepers working fifteen-hour days would get verbal and sometimes physical abuse.

As a result, Sikh immigrants would congregate in places like the temples, where they felt safe and where incidents like that didn't happen.

***

Politics is a fascination to me and I think you can see a lot of what was happening then being repeated now with attitudes towards Polish people. People are blaming foreigners for their problems and that's why we got Brexit. Fifty-six per cent of people in Luton voted to leave – 4 per cent above the national average. Even though the campaign was blatantly playing on a fear of immigrants, a third of the South Asian population also voted to leave. They'd integrated so successfully that they were now coming out with the same arguments that had been used against their parents a few decades earlier!

I think Brexit happened because the Brexiteers convinced so many people it was the right thing to 'get our country back'. Even though Britain was part of the EU, they felt EU nationals were coming to England and taking our jobs. It was exactly the same accusation they levelled at my parents' generation and not enough people pointed out the contributions they have made. It takes guts and determination to move to a foreign country and make a life for yourself; they were hard-working people who came here to contribute to British life.

I think Brexit was an enormous gamble and, in my opinion, even some of its campaigners were hoping that it wouldn't happen. They were using the campaign for their own political ambitions and assuming they wouldn't have to deliver on their promises. Now it's happened, they haven't got a clue how to make it work.

It could cost us billions to get divorced from the EU. Is it really worth it?

Chapter 3

'Just Two Sets of British People Fighting Each Other'

While the British Empire's overall legacy is chequered, they did give the world something that would eventually bring communities together and heal divisions: the game of cricket.

The racism of the post-war era was the reason we had clubs called Luton Caribbeans, Luton Pakistanis and Luton Indians. It was natural for expats to congregate in their own little communities and Luton Indians Cricket Club was formed so that the Indian émigrés could play cricket with their fellow Indians.

By the time I was growing up, attitudes were changing. Luton Town always used to be a white club and a lot of the players used to play Minor Counties cricket. They played at Wardown Park, which was the best ground in the area. It wasn't Lord's, but it had a smart pavilion, an old-school scorebox built into a clock, and a big, sweeping bank of concrete seating, which meant it could accommodate thousands of fans.

The international touring sides pulled the biggest crowds, but Luton Town used to get gates of 1,500 to 2,000 just for league games, and Northants regularly got double that when they used it for first class matches as one of their outgrounds.

If you played for Luton Town you were known as one of the top cricketers in Bedfordshire. It was a really high level, but by the time the millennium was approaching they were starting to run out of members. Luton Indians, by contrast, had a lot of members but didn't have great facilities. They played at Popes Meadow, which is just the other side of the river from Wardown Park, but very basic by comparison.

The solution was obvious: a white club and a brown club mixed to form Luton Town & Indians. Cricket was bringing people together.

***

It's an exaggeration to say that cricket had turned Luton into a multi-racial utopia, but by the 1980s it was a much easier place for a Sikh boy to grow up.

We lived in Stopsley, which used to be a village until it was swallowed up by Luton sometime before the war. For the first ten years of my life we lived at 232 Hitchin Road, an elegant-looking terraced house on a fairly steep hill. The house itself was several metres above the actual street level and we had to traipse up a set of concrete steps just to get to the front door. It was quite a busy road and the view out of the front windows was of more terraced houses and an industrial estate, but out the back there was a wooded copse-like area.

We never had problems with our white neighbours, perhaps because my mum used to invite them in to try her Indian specialities. My brother, sister and I would be killing ourselves laughing when these unsuspecting Luton boys and girls ate her samosas, because their mouths weren't used to the spices. They'd take a bite and then there'd be about a second before their cheeks would go red and we'd have to get them a glass of water. They'd get used to it. Indian food became so popular that at one point there were 17,000 Indian restaurants in England.

By then the white people were getting used to us and if they needed someone to hate, Watford was only 19 miles down the road. Luton/Watford was quite an intense rivalry for a while, although it was usually more about humour than violence.

There's a story about a Watford fan who told his daughter that trees couldn't grow in Bedfordshire. She believed him until she was at secondary school and saw an oak while on a geography field trip to Dunstable!

Kenilworth Road was seen as the gritty, intimidating venue, a really old ground packed into a working-class area with a hard, plastic pitch that every visiting side hated, whilst Watford were supposed to be the friendliest club in England. Luton fans would argue that in this context the word 'friendliest' actually meant 'least atmospheric'. Even the name, Vicarage Road, implies it's a home for retired clergymen, and the ground was full of middle-class fans who made so little noise they eventually had to pipe artificial crowd chants through the PA system.

If you were a Luton fan who liked Elton John, you had to tape his songs off the radio because you knew if you bought the actual record, the money was helping to build their new stand!

In the year I was born, Luton beat Watford to the Division Two title by eight points and they stayed in the top flight for most of the next decade. I was too young to remember this golden age, although I've obviously seen the footage from 1983, with David Pleat running onto the pitch at Maine

Road, after Raddy Antic had scored the goal that kept us up while sending Man City down.

I've also heard the stories about the Millwall FA Cup quarter-final in 1985. If you watch the footage now it looks more like a medieval battle than a football match, with 10,000 Millwall fans crammed into an area that had a capacity of 5,000 and hanging off fences with metal spikes and floodlight pylons.

Luton won 1-0 and at the final whistle you can see the players literally running for their lives. The police fought what was literally a pitch battle with hundreds of Millwall fans who were hurling plastic seats at them, and outside the ground fans were sacking the streets nearby, hurling bricks and concrete through living room windows and windscreens.

These boys did not discriminate on racial grounds: white, black or Asian, they were coming after you.

For about a week, Luton became the centre of the universe. There was an emergency debate in Parliament; one MP said they should bring back the birch and the Luton Chairman, David Evans, nearly went into orbit.

Evans was also the Tory MP for Welwyn and Hatfield, and he'd apparently been a very good opening batsman who'd been at Warwickshire and Gloucestershire, although he'd never made it into their first teams. He was a real firebrand, the type of MP who'd probably have hung the hooligans from the floodlights if he'd been given the chance. He banned away fans from Kenilworth Road, which, along with our plastic pitch, helped make Luton one of the most hated sides in the country.

The weird thing is, although it was only a couple of miles away, the riot didn't really affect us. People who lived in Kenilworth Road were getting their cars torched and bricks through their living room windows, but it was 2 miles from Stopsley. You wouldn't have known anything had happened until you picked up the newspapers the following morning or switched on the TV and saw Mrs Thatcher demanding to know why Luton had been razed to the ground.

To us it was just two sets of British people fighting each other! Whenever that happened, we'd be like, why are they getting that upset over a football game?

I think football hooligan culture was for the working-class men who worked hard shifts, in the coal mines up north and the factories down here. Saturday was a time for them to really let go of pent-up energy and connect it to the sport. They were fighting each other to show their passion and being a hooligan was another way to get that buzz out of the game.

I never experienced anything like that on a cricket field, although Hitu Naik, my coach and mentor, took me to the Under-15 World Cup final at Lord's between India and Pakistan when I was still a kid, and that got unexpectedly lively.

India had Mohammed Kaif, and even at that age you could see he was an extremely good player. Hitu said, 'Let's watch these players and see where we are by comparison.'

I couldn't believe how good they were. They'd hit the ball so hard and they ran between the wickets like they were already professional cricketers. It was amazing to watch but when India won, both teams ran on the field and fighting broke out!

I think India v Pakistan games are the closest thing we get to football hooliganism, although it's a bit of a myth that cricket's a gentlemen's game, where everyone shakes hands at stumps and shares a beer. That does happen, but you do get fights as well. All these guys that go to the gym and take steroids, they have to release their energy somehow and they release it during the India v Pakistan games. It's The India Steroid Boys against The Pakistani Steroid boys!

***

The India v Pakistan rivalry was another legacy of the British Empire.

Muslims and Hindus had coexisted peacefully on the sub-continent in the past, but in the twentieth century, nationalism was increasing and the British solution was not to encourage people to learn to live with each other but to create two separate countries.

When India was given independence in 1947, Pakistan was formed as a separate, supposedly Muslim state, but millions of people were trapped on the 'wrong' side of the new borders. The idea of a partition was too simplistic and the new governments were completely unprepared for the sectarian hell it unleashed. The British didn't help by bringing independence forward by a year.

Violence erupted. Muslims living in India and Hindus stuck in Pakistan felt they had to leave. A million people died, some through violence but many through the diseases that were spreading through the totally inadequate refugee camps.

When the wave of South Asian immigrants first came to Luton there was a lot of hostility between Indians and Pakistanis, but they started to amalgamate because they'd do business with each other, play against each other and eventually become friends with each other. A lot of the construction work my dad gets now comes from Pakistani clients.

There's an irony for the ages. The British Empire didn't think we could live together on the sub-continent but when we got to Luton, everyone chilled out and got on with their lives.

***

Another irony of my childhood is that I became an Arsenal supporter, given that I was only six when they suffered one of their greatest humiliations, at the hands of Luton Town. Again, I've obviously seen replays of the 1988 League Cup final, but at the time I probably didn't even know it was on.

Arsenal were 2-1 up with ten minutes left when Andy Dibble saved a penalty from Nigel Winterburn. Danny Wilson equalised two minutes later, and Brian Stein got a winner in the last minute after Tony Adams gave away a free kick. Stein and Dibble are folk heroes in Luton and even thirty years later, fans talk about it as if it happened yesterday. The greatest era in the history of Luton Town coincided with my formative years, and I don't remember any of it!

By the time I'd started taking an interest in football, Luton had been relegated and Arsenal were the nearest Premier League side. George Graham was the manager and I can still reel that team off the top of my head: David Seaman in goal, then Lee Dixon, Steve Bould, Tony Adams and Nigel Winterburn at the back, with David O'Leary and Andy Linighan covering; in midfield you had David Rocastle, Michael Thomas, Paul Davis and David Hillier. Anders Limpar was on the wing and up front it was Paul Merson, Alan Smith and later, Ian Wright. Later still, you had the French Foreign Legion, plus Marc Overmars and Dennis Bergkamp.

A lot of my knowledge derives from a sticker album and a minor act of larceny. I used to walk to school via a shop that belonged to the father of a friend of mine, Amish Gandhi (he's now a qualified doctor). Amish's dad had a newsagent's on the High Town Road and I was probably his best customer. I'd buy stickers with a £5 note I'd taken from my dad's pocket. I did it once and he didn't notice, so I tried it again. If he had any loose change I'd take it and spend it on stickers, first football and then WWF wrestling, which became another obsession.

My favourite was The Undertaker. He was well over 2 metres tall and because he wore a hat, he looked even bigger. He had hair that always looked wet and a facial expression that said he was going to bury you. He wasn't there to enjoy it, which was why he never smiled. It was just his job. I'd later meet a few cricketers who were like that, especially coaches.

The Ultimate Warrior looked like a rock musician, and then you had Hulk Hogan. The two of them would just fling people out of the ring and when that had finished, WrestleMania would come on with Brett 'the Hitman' Hart, the Legion of Doom and Jake the Snake, who used to come onto the stage brandishing his cobra. He looked a bit like my future Bedfordshire teammate Wayne Larkins, or at least he would have done if Wayne had put on a few stone and developed a fondness for purple spandex.

I loved the theatricality of it all, but what made it even more attractive for kids was the sticker collection. Swapping stickers was a great way of making friends in the school playground, because you could stand around and yell, 'Who's got Rick Blair?'

Dad never noticed that his money was disappearing. Even now, I don't think he realises; he probably just thinks he had holes in his pockets.

Eventually a buzz started to build around Luton Town again when they got to the semi-finals of the FA Cup in 1994, and this was when I started to take an interest. David Pleat was back in charge and he'd got a great team together, which included John Hartson and Kerry Dixon up front. They'd started playing the semi-finals at Wembley a few years earlier and we'd beaten West Ham and Newcastle to get that far. However, on the day itself we never really got going, losing 2-0 to Chelsea.

They went on to become one of the biggest clubs in Europe and we ended up in the Conference! I stuck with Luton, though. Some people say you can't support two clubs, but most people who follow local sides in the smaller towns also follow a Premier League team.

I don't think Arsenal have played Luton since I started supporting them both. If they ever did, I'd probably have to cut the shirt down the middle and have half in red and half in orange!

Chapter 4

The Cricket Test

I was blissfully unaware of a lot of things when I was eight years old. One of them was Norman Tebbit. He was a Conservative MP who'd held Cabinet rank and had been chairman of his party when Margaret Thatcher was Prime Minister.

In 1990, he gave an interview to the *Los Angeles Times* in which he said: 'A large proportion of Britain's Asian population fail to pass the cricket test. Which side do they cheer for? Are you still harking back to where you came from or where you are?'

He later claimed this was a plea for integration, but it didn't sound like it at the time. No one ever asked this question about Australian or New Zealand cricket fans who lived in England, so why was he singling out the Asians? Was he really that upset about them supporting India or Pakistan at Lord's or was there something else he was angry about?

A Labour MP called Jeff Rooker claimed Tebbit knew exactly what he was doing and said he should be prosecuted for inciting racial hatred. Paddy Ashdown, who was then the leader of the Liberal Democrats, called on Mrs Thatcher to condemn the remarks. She ignored him. Tebbit had a track record of saying provocative things about people who didn't enjoy the luxury of white skin. He'd called anti-apartheid campaigners hypocrites and opposed a scheme to allow 250,000 Hong Kong residents to come to Britain, the country that then 'owned' Hong Kong as one of its last colonies.

Of course, the moment anyone said, 'You know, Norman, don't you think that might be a little bit racist?' you could guess the reaction from his supporters.

'Racist? That's an outrageous thing to say! It's political correctness gone mad.'

This was the response of one *Daily Telegraph* reader:

Sir,
The fuss over Norman Tebbit's so-called 'cricket test' put me in mind of a simple method of testing the allegiance of foreigners. My old school, Hadleigh's, had its share of exotic creatures even in the 1920s, and all boys were put through a 'cricket test' that left no

room for doubt. One by one, we stood in front of the wicket with our hands behind our backs while the First XI bowlers sent down their fastest deliveries, aimed just below the waist. No protective boxes were allowed, and any boy who stood firm was 'in'. Colour didn't come into it.

Cedric Lawton
Esher, Surrey

So even in interwar England, the game was being used as a force for the integration of 'exotic creatures'. You just had to stand still while a fast bowler tried to circumcise you using a cricket ball.

You can imagine Mr Lawton sitting on the boundary rope at Hadleigh's saying, 'You know that darkie's not a bad chap really. The bowler was aiming right at his goolies and he didn't move a muscle. I think he might be one of us.' And if he was still alive today, I dare say he'd claim to be horrified at any suggestion that this was somehow racist.

***

The irony of all this is that my dad is exactly the kind of entrepreneurial man Tebbit claimed to admire, someone who, like his own father, 'got on his bike' and looked for work during a recession. (In a further irony, Tebbit would later blame cyclists for air pollution during a debate in the House of Lords and inevitably he got annoyed when one of his fellow peers heckled him with a cry of 'Get on your bike.')

Dad was someone who had the courage to move to a foreign country, hold down a full-time job, support his wife and three children and still study for his A levels in the evenings. That must have been exhausting, but he still had the energy to play cricket at the weekends.

He was an all-rounder who used to play for Luton Tech College and he would just hit the ball ... hit the ball all day. I used to be their scorer and I remember he got hit in the eye once and was cut so badly that he needed stitches. He wasn't a bad little cricketer but after a while he stopped, because he'd started his own business as a carpenter. He's well known in the town for his work in the construction industry and in keeping with the idea of Sikh families adopting English nicknames, we call him Bob the Builder.

We watched programmes that the white English kids watched, like *The Pink Panther* and *Inspector Gadget*, and we grew up with an English sense of humour, partly because we watched programmes like *Dad's Army* and *Only*

Fools and Horses. That was classic English comedy. It was really funny, but it was all about people's habits, with an underlying streak of sadness. In *Dad's Army* there was always gentle humour, even though in the background they knew they were facing a fight for their very survival.

Only Fools and Horses was about the fight for survival in a way, but it was also about aspiration. They were three men working hard because they dreamed of a better life. Sikhs who came to England could identify with that.

So we integrated pretty well, while retaining our links to our heritage. My parents insisted I attend Punjabi language classes and I didn't always want to go, but I'm grateful I did because I'm now fluent in three languages: English, Punjabi and Hindi. I'm quite fluent in Urdu, which is a similar dialect to Punjabi and Hindi, and I also got a C for my French GCSE. I'm not fluent, but I can still speak a bit of French when needed, which admittedly isn't often on the international circuit.

***

I was oblivious to all the undertones of the cricket test because when the story broke I was still at primary school. In our community everyone thought we should support England, so we did. If they weren't playing, I supported India and it didn't occur to me that there might be anything morally dubious about it. I just loved cricket and by the time of the 1992 World Cup, I was becoming obsessed.

I started as a left-arm seamer, because I wanted to be Wasim Akram. This was when I was first becoming aware of Sachin Tendulkar, who'd become my hero, but I admired a lot of the players at that tournament, regardless of where they came from. Mark Greatbatch would come in and smash it like no one else could and the New Zealand team that got to the semi-finals had a lot of great players, like Ken Rutherford and Chris Harris. I loved Danny Morrison's action. I don't remember too much about the Australian side as it was one of the few tournaments when they failed, but I can remember David Boon because he looked so distinctive with his moustache.

The real icon, however, was Wasim. It was the first tournament when coloured uniforms were used. It wasn't easy to look cool in a pair of lime green pyjamas, but he somehow managed it.

Pakistan didn't start the tournament well but they just did enough to qualify for the last four and saw off New Zealand in the semi-finals. In a close final, Wasim was the difference. Most people remember him for his bowling, but he was an explosive batsman as well, and Pakistan were in real trouble when he came in and smacked 33 from eighteen balls. They made 249-6, which looks low by today's standards but back then was probably a halfway house kind of score.

It was gettable, but Wasim struck early, getting Ian Botham for a duck, caught behind. England recovered well with Allan Lamb and Neil Fairbrother, who was batting without a helmet, which seems unbelievable now. They'd pulled it back to 141-4 when Imran decided it was time for his not-so-secret weapon.

I'd never seen anyone do the things to a cricket ball that Wasim did and when he took two wickets with two deliveries, it absolutely killed England. The way he celebrated bowling Allan Lamb was unforgettable. He bowled left arm around the wicket and Lamb was expecting it to swing, so he prodded at it. Instead the ball held its line and smashed his off stump. Wasim ran forward with his arms aloft, pumping them in sheer joy before he high-fived Moin Khan.

He actually looked a bit like David Pleat at Maine Road, and maybe that's where he got the idea! For a moment he seemed to be almost overwhelmed and then the expression on his face changed, because he knew the job wasn't quite done. With the very next ball he got Chris Lewis to play on. This time the ball pitched wider outside off stump. Lewis went after it, but this delivery did swing and Lewis steered it into his stumps. And this time, Wasim allowed himself to lose it, because England were six down and 108 runs adrift with only fifteen overs to go. By today's standards, a run rate of 7.5 an over wasn't impossible, but in that era it just didn't happen.

Later that summer, Pakistan came to England, with a bowler who was almost Wasim's equal and who hadn't even played in that final. Waqar Younis was one of the greatest bowlers of all time. When he and Wasim were in tandem it was frightening, but captivating to watch. I wanted England to win, but at the same time I was in awe of the pair of them and they way they could reverse swing the ball so it homed in on the foot of the stumps, or crushed the batsmen's toes, almost like heat-seeking missiles.

Even at that age I knew some people were questioning how they could do it without ball tampering. The accusations finally came into the open during a one-dayer at Lord's when England were chasing 205 to win. This was the era when one-dayers could spill over into a second day if it rained, and England were 140-5 at lunch on day two when the umpires decided to change the ball because it looked like it had been gouged.

You could, however, always rely on Geoffrey Boycott to put things in perspective. After Wasim and Waqar had taken the ungouged replacement ball and skittled England, he said: 'Pakistan could have bowled England out with an orange.'

It was all too much for Allan Lamb, who gave the *Daily Mirror* an exclusive with an article subtly headlined 'How Pakistan cheat at cricket'. The *Mirror* splashed it all over the front page and it escalated from there. Imran reacted by making accusations against Lamb and Ian Botham, which culminated in them all ending up in court four years later. Lamb and Botham sued Imran Khan for libel and lost, although apparently even Imran seemed stunned.

And I watched it all unfold, still completely oblivious that a dozen years later, I'd find myself embroiled in a Pakistan ball-tampering scandal that would make this one look tame.

***

Although I was obsessed by cricket as a 10-year-old, I wasn't always that keen on actually playing it. My dad sometimes had to drag me to the games and on one occasion, maybe the first time I'd played, I can remember actually crying in the car. I'm not sure why I was so upset, but I do remember that I'd cheered up significantly when I started taking wickets. That was a great feeling. You'd get someone out and all of a sudden you'd have people running towards you, smiling and patting you on the back. A bowler never loses that sensation. I always liked making people happy!

That's the upside of being a bowler. You can make a stadium full of 90,000 people erupt with a single delivery. The downside is that if things are going badly, you're stuck out there. A batsman is only ever one ball away from dismissal, but if he does get out he's at least spared any further punishment.

When I was at Bedford School we went on a tour to Barbados and ended up in the same bar as Brian Lara. I spent half an hour grilling him about cricket and he listened to me, an unknown schoolboy, politely before finally extricating himself with the words: 'Maybe we'll play against each other one day.'

Part of me is glad I didn't. Ask Gareth Batty how much fun it was bowling fifty-two overs and ending up with figures of 2-185 when he made his world record 400 not out.

Geoff Boycott used to say the best way to deal with fast bowling was from the other end. The best way to deal with Brian Lara's batting? Wait until he retires before becoming an international bowler.

Gordon Greenidge, whom I'd later play with for Lashings, was another player I met while I was still a kid. His most memorable piece of advice was that if I ever stopped enjoying cricket, I should stop. Gordon was still playing well into his sixties, flicking the ball off his hips like a man a third of his age, and still enjoying it.

Once I'd overcome my initial stage fright, it never occurred to me that I'd stop enjoying cricket. Or that one day I'd contemplate giving it all up in the middle of an Ashes series.

Chapter 5

Straight Outta Stopsley

Between them, my father and Hitu Naik ensured that I struck the right balance between studying and cricket, and I was lucky that I had good schools to go to.

As a junior I went to St Matthew's in Stopsley. It was a happy school; the infants and juniors were right next to each other and I can remember playing the Hairy Fairy when we did *Cinderella* as the school panto. I didn't have any lines but acting's something I've always been interested in. I could do impressions at a young age. We had a teacher there called Mr Charles, who somehow found the time to smoke twenty fags a day. He was a maths teacher who had a big, crooked nose, smoky skin, browny sort of hair and a husky voice. He always had a mint in his mouth to try to mask the smell of the cigarettes but it didn't work: whenever he breathed you caught wind of a mixture of tobacco and mint.

I'd make people laugh by copying him and even now I like to act in different ways around my family, pretending to be serious or maybe winding them up to try to get a reaction. I can do quite an accurate impression of David Lloyd, although 'Bomble' is himself one of the best impressionists on the cricket circuit. He can do everyone; he picks up the accent straight away and launches into a routine. The first time I met him I was with Chris Tremlett and he was absolutely cracking up. We'd ask him to do Bob Willis or David Gower and he'd say, 'I'm not a purrforming monkeh, here for your enturtaaaynmunt.'

Acting might be something I'll look at once the cricket's over. I wouldn't mind being a cricketing version of Eric Cantona. I do have a passion for it. I quite like Brad Pitt because he plays so many different roles: he plays the funny roles like Aldo Raine in *Inglourious Basterds* and the gangster roles like Tyler Durden in *Fight Club*. I also like Denzel Washington, who I think is a very talented actor. I used to like *House of Cards* and Kevin Spacey, but when the news broke about what he got up to off-screen it all felt a bit weird.

From St Matthew's I went to Stopsley High School, which already had its fair share of famous alumni. The actor Rodney Bewes, who starred in *The Likely Lads*, went there, as did Bruce Rioch, who played for Scotland in the 1978 World Cup and later managed Arsenal for a season. The television presenter Stacey Dooley also went there, although she was a few years after me.

I spent five years at Stopsley and emerged with four As, four Bs and two Cs when I took my GCSEs, at which point I found myself at a fork in the road. The easiest thing to do would have been to stay on in Luton and go to a sixth-form college, but I was playing for Luton Indians and some of my mates were going to Bedford Modern, about forty-five minutes away up the A6. It was a fee-paying school, but they took me on a two-year sports scholarship because by then I was playing Minor Counties cricket for Bedfordshire.

***

I was about twelve when I realised I was maybe better than average at cricket, and it was Paul Taylor who noticed something that everyone else had missed, during a coaching session for one of Bedfordshire's youth teams.

Taylor was a tall, left-arm fast bowler who enjoyed seventeen years as a county pro and had recently endured England's 1993 tour of India, where he'd played a single Test on a dead pitch in Kolkata. He'd watched me trying to impersonate Wasim Akram and noticed how accurate I was.

Taylor sidled over and said, 'Why don't you try putting some spin on it?'

I tried it and was fairly happy with the results, but I still wasn't sure I was ready to give up on my dream of being Luton's answer to Wasim. For the next two seasons I was a bit like a bowling all-rounder, trying seam and spin, but I decided to concentrate on the latter when I took 7-35, bowling only spin for Bedfordshire Under-15s against Worcestershire.

There was never a level where I thought I might struggle, and I always seemed to be ahead of the game. At fifteen I played against 19-year-olds, at sixteen, I was playing Minor Counties cricket. The game doesn't change. The difference is that in Minor Counties cricket, three out of six balls will land. In first class cricket it's four out of six, and at international level it's usually five. (Or six, if you're unlucky enough to be facing someone like Glenn McGrath.)

I have to confess, I didn't really follow county cricket until I started playing for Northants, but this might have worked in my favour because I didn't get overawed when I moved up through the levels. Although I'd met a few professionals, like Greenidge and Taylor, the first time I actually played alongside one was when I made my first team debut for Bedfordshire alongside Wayne Larkins. He did not look like your average cricketer. Earlier in his career he'd looked like the comedian Bobby Ball, with his big curly hair and his moustache. Now his hair had grown longer and he looked like a Cavalier from the Civil War era.

Wayne didn't take his cricket too seriously. In fact, he didn't seem to take his life too seriously, and that would frequently get him into trouble. He'd have a pint before going in to bat, then smash the ball everywhere with his big, strong forearms. I called it his Ian Botham mode.

I didn't drink at the time, so I had no idea what effect the alcohol might have had on him, but a lot of people thought he hadn't realised his full potential as a cricketer. You could argue that if he'd gone out to bat sober, he would have been an even better player, but he felt it relaxed him and it hadn't exactly done Beefy any harm. Wayne was also a chain-smoker, though, and it was for that reason that Graham Gooch took the visionary decision to ask him to share a room with a fellow smoker, the young Phil Tufnell, on England's tour to Australia in 1990–91. You can imagine how well that worked out!

By then Wayne had been in and out of the England side for the best part of a decade. He'd been so annoyed at being left out of the tour to India in 1981–82 that he went on the rebel tour to South Africa instead, not realising that if he'd stayed put he could have walked into the real England team in place of Gooch, Boycott or any of the other players who'd made themselves ineligible. Instead, he served a three-year international ban, during which he 'Nedded' the county bowlers so effectively that they had to recall him when he'd done his time.

He was thirty-seven by the time he was rooming with Tuffers. He sat next to him on the plane to Perth, plied him with booze and then made him raid the team's storeroom at the hotel before they'd even checked into their room. Tuffers said that Gooch eventually tracked them down and found them in a cloud of smoke, with the empty cans already piling high. He ordered them downstairs to go for a training run.

Even in that state, Tuffers was just about together enough to know it wasn't a great idea to ignore a direct order from his captain, but when he asked Wayne if he was coming along, he just said he was 'right as rain' where he was and carried on drinking without him. Tuffers found him in their room eight hours later, watching TV, still smoking, and building a pyramid of empty cans.

And he still averaged 23.5 on the tour!

He was well into his forties by the time I met him but even though he was over twice my age, I liked him straight away. The first thing he said to me was: 'You remind me of Bishan Bedi.' Maybe it was an obvious comparison because I was wearing a patka, but who wouldn't like being compared to a legend like Bedi? It was Bedi on whom I'd modelled myself. I'd studied his action in the MCC coaching manual and he was beautifully light on his feet.

Wayne was also a gentleman. Although he was still drinking like he had holes in his feet, he wasn't the kind of belligerent boozer who'd get offended if you refused to have a drink with him. If I said I was sticking to soft drinks, he accepted it immediately and never made an issue of it – which is probably just as well given that I was both teetotal and underage at the time.

Years later, Wayne got involved in a mortgage scam when his girlfriend forged her own father's signature so they could buy a holiday home in France. They got away with a twelve-month suspended sentence and 200 hours of community service, but even then, Wayne couldn't help himself. He didn't bother turning up for community service. He didn't contact his supervision officer and he didn't bother telling the court he'd changed address. After five no-shows they issued a warrant for his arrest and he handed himself in to the police before throwing himself at the mercy of the court.

The judge said he wasn't entitled to any special treatment because he was a cricketer. He then gave him special treatment because he was a cricketer.

The defence argued that Wayne hadn't acted out of any malice but had been guilty of putting his head in the sand. The prosecution accepted that and said he deserved a final chance. The judge agreed. Wayne did the work and avoided jail.

Chapter 6

The Only Way is Northants

I was sixteen years and 113 days old when I made my Minor Counties debut for Bedfordshire, making me their youngest ever first team player, although that didn't really mean a lot to me at the time.

I didn't want to be the best spin bowler in Luton. I didn't want to be the best spin bowler in Bedfordshire. I wanted to be The Greatest Spin Bowler in the World, and that became my mantra.

I want to be The Greatest Spin Bowler in the World.
I want to be The Greatest Spin Bowler in the World.
I want to be The Greatest Spin Bowler in the World.

Unfortunately, I was so oblivious as to the way cricket worked, I didn't have a clue how to get there. I just assumed it involved playing for England. Looking back, I was on the right road, even if I didn't realise it.

By the time I made my Bedfordshire debut I'd already become the subject of what the tabloids might call a 'bidding war' between Essex and Northamptonshire. Essex saw me first. Hitu, who had a significantly better idea of the road map from club cricketer to The Greatest Spin Bowler in the World than I did, used to tell me I needed to make an extra effort when playing against youth teams from first class counties because they'd always have a scout watching.

I did well against Essex Under-17s and was approached by a tall, distinguished looking gentlemen in an Essex tracksuit.

'Hi, nice to meet you, I'm John Childs.'

'Hi, I'm Monty Panesar. I want to be The Greatest Spin Bowler in the World.'

Childs was England's oldest post-war Test debutant, winning his first cap when he was thirty-six. As I'm thirty-six at the time of writing this book, he is now a source of ongoing inspiration to me, but at the time I had absolutely no idea who he was. He did, however, ask me to come to Chelmsford for a trial, which was one way of getting on my good side.

The trial in question got off to the worst possible start because we had an indoor net in which Graham Napier drove the ball back at such speed I thought it might take my hand off. I stupidly tried to field it and felt a level of pain I'd never previously experienced on the cricket field. When I looked down I was surprised I didn't have a hole where my palm was. I felt like crying but through the pain I realised that wasn't a good look for someone who wanted to be The Greatest Spin Bowler in the World, so I just smiled and took it.

Things could only get better after that, and they did. As soon as we got outdoors they could see my potential. They thought I was ready for second and even first team cricket almost immediately, but they didn't offer me a deal. They just wanted me to keep coming back, join the group and keep on bowling.

It was all a bit weird, because they knew Northants were interested as well. At the end of the session Childs came up to me and said, 'I know what Northants will do, they'll offer you a summer contract.'

Which they did.

Northants were the 'local' county. Their coaching set-up had a direct link with Bedfordshire and they used Wardown Park as an outground, so people from Luton usually supported them. I didn't, but that was because at the time I had only a slim idea of what county cricket actually was.

We drove up to Wantage Road, which had to be one of the most unusual cricket grounds in the country. It was crammed into the middle of a high-density residential area, surrounded by red-brick terraced housing that made it look more like Kenilworth Road than Lord's. It looked like a football ground. I later found out that this was because it was a football ground: Northampton Town had played there until 1994.

I went inside and met a man called Steve Coverdale, who had slightly thinning brown hair that hung over his ears in clumps, a bit like Terry Wogan's. He took me to his office and introduced himself as the club's chief executive. In lieu of an introduction, I told him I wanted to be The Greatest Spin Bowler in the World. He seemed slightly taken aback, though he recovered his composure and suggested that the best way of achieving this might be to sign for Northants.

'But I want to be The Greatest Spin Bowler in the World.'

'And?'

'How can I be The Greatest Spin Bowler in the World if I'm only playing for Northants? I want to play for England. I don't want to be bound to this.'

Steve paused for a second. Looking back I imagine that was the time it took him to realise that I wasn't actually winding him up. I had quite an earnest facial expression and my big saucer eyes probably convinced him I was genuine. Steve patiently explained that not only was it possible to play for both a county team and England, it would be extremely difficult to do it any other way. Paul Taylor had done it after all, as had Allan Lamb, albeit via a slightly different route.

'So I can play for you and England?'

'Yes.'

'Oh, right. I didn't know that.'

It turned out that I wasn't necessarily the most naive person in the room. A couple of years later, Steve left Northants after £247,000 went missing from the club's accounts. He hadn't taken it, but as the club's chief executive he hadn't been performing due diligence and didn't notice the shortfall. An employee called Sue Woodward had been forging his signature and Steve hadn't noticed that her lifestyle seemed slightly extravagant for someone who was earning £14,000 a year.

'Going anywhere nice for your holidays, Sue?'

'Yeah, taking the family to Vegas.'

'Oh, that's nice. Not going to the second home in Marbella this time?'

'No. Maybe next year.'

Sue was the co-signatory to all the club's bank accounts. In the space of five months, from November 2002 to March 2003, she'd cashed seventy-seven fake cheques, either to her own bank accounts or to her credit cards; £1,900 went to Harrods and over £9,000 to M&S. The defence said she did it because she was inexperienced and couldn't cope with the pressure of the job. She pleaded guilty to nineteen charges of theft and asked for fifty-eight other offences to be taken into consideration. The judge sentenced her to twenty months in prison. My guess is, Wayne Larkins had a better legal team.

***

In purely cricketing terms there was nothing between Northants and Essex. They both had excellent facilities and a roster of great players. The only difference was the geography. Wantage Road was under an hour away up the M1 and Chelmsford was nearly double that across country.

Everything Childs predicted would happen did happen. They offered me a summer contract and I signed it, purely because Wantage Road was nearer. In terms of facilities there was nothing in it and I thought both Childs and

Nick Cook at Northants were both great coaches, but it was just that much easier to get to Wantage Road.

In hindsight, maybe I should have thought about Essex's track record in producing England cricketers. Nasser Hussain was there, as was Graham Gooch. Keith Fletcher was on the staff and Alastair Cook was coming through. These were greats of the game and their influence might have seen me selected for England earlier. I might even be sitting with Nasser right now, in the Sky Sports commentary box!

For whatever reason, Northants just hadn't produced as many internationals of the same stature, although with Graeme Swann and me on the books that was about to change.

***

My summer contract was worth £2,000 and my only previous employment, if you could call it that, had been knocking on doors for Anglia Windows and getting a fiver in commission if I generated a lead. I ended up spending the money on ice creams and other stuff so I don't think I made more than about £500 in the two or three months I was doing it. It was the sort of job where people would regularly tell you to 'fuck off' if you weren't careful, so I usually picked a nice area in Dunstable where people were generally polite. The problem was it was stultifyingly dull. If ever I needed an additional incentive to become The Greatest Spin Bowler in the World it was the fear of having to walk round the back streets of Dunstable trying to flog replacement windows.

The challenge was to try to break into the first team while still completing my A levels, because once I'd realised that 17-year-olds didn't just walk into county first teams, I knew I'd need to have something to fall back other than a career in the Dunstable glazing industry.

Northants agreed and my 2nd XI debut was delayed until July, when we played Warwickshire in a one-dayer at Leamington Spa. We lost heavily, but I'd at least taken a wicket and Wayne Larkins had turned up to watch, which meant a lot to me. To this day, I've nothing but love for Ned.

A week later, I took 5-114 in a three-day win over Surrey at Milton Keynes. I was starting to feel like a professional cricketer. I just wasn't starting to look like one. I was still using a plastic bag to carry my equipment and my helmet was so large that the opposition fielders called me a starship trooper.

A year later, I'd completed my A levels (three Bs, in Chemistry, Maths and Physics) and been selected for the England Under-19s alongside Ian Bell, Chris Tremlett and Gary Pratt.

The first time I saw Ian Bell I thought he had everything. He just looked so immaculate. I remember seeing him play for Warwickshire against either Northants or the MCC at Dunstable, and even then I'd rock up in a tracksuit while he'd turn up in a blazer and pressed trousers. If you're going to turn up looking like that you have to be a good player. He scored a double hundred.

At the time he looked like a future England captain. I can remember he once called me into a room because I'd been messing around on a tour bus with Ian Pattison and we'd got into a bit of a water fight that got slightly out of hand. I think he was supposed to be bollocking me but I didn't take in a word he said because I was so amazed by the state of his room. It was the sort of place where you didn't want to sit down because you were worried you might leave a dent on the cushions.

He was a prodigy. He was always putting himself under pressure but he was absolutely beautiful to watch. Whenever I bowled at him in the nets he always used to come down the wicket and hit me for six. I think I was his checkpoint, to see if his feet were moving correctly and his balance was right. In all the years I bowled at him in net sessions I think I might have got him stumped about twice. He was also an unbelievably good short leg fielder. Only he'll know why he was never really in the running for the top job, but I'd say the difference between him and Ricky Ponting is that Ricky always had a bit more of an edge about him. He was a fighter whilst Ian was a technician.

As a number three batsman I think Ian had even better technique than Ricky, but he wouldn't put himself forward in the dressing room, and to be a captain you've got to give your opinions. By contrast, Alastair Cook was never shy about expressing his thoughts and leadership was just a natural progression for him.

If I'd been selected for England's Under-19s, I had to be doing something right, but in hindsight I was painfully naive about how the system worked. I assumed Northants was an easy stepping stone to England, just as Bedfordshire had been a stepping stone to Northants.

In one of my first games, Rob Bailey was fielding at slip. He came up to me at the end of an over and said, 'You're ready for first team cricket, mate.' First, however, I had to get university out of the way.

Chapter 7

The Top Two Things to do in Loughborough

There was a reason why so many top sports stars had emerged from Loughborough University. There was nothing else to do in Lougborough.

Most of the major UK universities were in big cities with multiple distractions – dreaming spires, punts, art galleries, night clubs and concert venues.

Loughborough had a bell tower.

If you type 'things to do in Loughborough' into a search engine, the response is almost apologetic. TripAdvisor's writer was asked to come up with a top ten, but he got stuck at two and was reduced to writing: 'We found some great things to do, but some are outside the town ...'

It's actually surrounded by Agnewshire, where you'll find some of the nicest countryside in England, but it's not the kind of town where you're going to get woken up at 5 am in the morning by students who've had a big night out, and I stayed in Harry French Court, a student residential hall that looked a bit like a sheltered housing area from the outside.

My favourite place in Loughborough was the Power Base gym on the campus, although the competition for that accolade wasn't fierce: it was that or the pizza parlour, where I could get a slice of Margherita for £1.99.

I've always loved 'the' gym and even now I think I'll always enjoy working out there, but this one looked more like an aircraft hanger and it was the kind of place you'd find England rugby players and Olympic athletes. I used to love lifting weights there and I was in awe of how fit some of the other gym-goers were. I'd think, how do people even exist like this?

Not everyone you meet there is exactly what they seem, however, even in provincial gyms. I can remember a coach telling me that he could always tell who was juicing because of their musculature. They weren't even athletes; just people who wanted to look good. After a while you can pick up on the telltale signs, although I have to say it isn't something I've ever come across in cricket. It's such a skill-driven sport that you don't necessarily get runs or take wickets from being big and strong.

Drug testing in cricket is usually there to detect performance-impairing substances, not performance enhancing ones. There have been a handful of cases of cricketers taking steroids and it's amazing how often they do it by 'accident' after taking a herbal remedy, but the only really high-profile doping case was when Shane Warne was banned for taking a diuretic, which he'd taken to lose weight. That didn't put him in the Lance Armstrong category.

If I'd been at a university like Bristol or Manchester, things might have worked out differently because of all the other distractions, but at Loughborough, I could concentrate on my cricket, especially as the ECB had just opened a Centre of Excellence there.

That, at least, was the theory. In reality, I lacked discipline. I always had a great training ethic and was happy to practise for hours on end, but I let myself down in other areas like punctuality. This is still a problem for me even now, although I have improved a lot.

The late Graham Dilley was the cricket coach. I should have been trying to make a good impression on him because he was also working with Nasser Hussain and Duncan Fletcher in the England set-up. Instead I let him down. He was a big fan of my bowling, but he wasn't a big fan of the way I'd be late for things, or of the way I'd turn up in my three-grand Hyundai Accent, which had nice wheels and a great sound system, but drained my bank balance because so many things kept going wrong with it.

I think Graham indulged me because he knew I had talent, but I wish I'd been more respectful of what he was trying to do at the time and now, of course, it's too late to apologise. He died of oesophageal cancer in 2011 at the age of fifty-two, just a week after being diagnosed. It was a shockingly young age to go for someone who had so much to offer.

***

If you'd seen the food I used to live off at Loughborough you'd have been amazed I ever ended up on *Celebrity MasterChef*. Like a lot of students who've moved away from home for the first time, I didn't have a clue how to cook. I lived off beans on toast for a while until I realised I needed to vary my diet and started eating at the canteen.

At that point I didn't have time for romantic relationships. When I wasn't playing cricket I was reading Computer Studies and Management, and when the exams came around, I approached them with the same level of calm I'd later bring to my fielding.

Playing for the university cricket team consumed a lot of the time I might otherwise have had for studying and I always seemed to end up cramming for exams. The realisation I needed to start preparing usually kicked in about two weeks beforehand and a cold fear would run through me. I'd take a look at the syllabus and wonder how the hell I'd be able to learn even a fraction of it. For the next fortnight I'd arrange the modules using colour codes, absorb as much information about each as I could, and then eventually fall asleep while trying to work out which topics were likely to come up. The actual exams were usually OK, after the initial shock had faded. For the first five minutes I'd be tense, but once I realised I knew what I was talking about and that the hours I'd put in had been worthwhile, I started to relax.

I eventually graduated with a 2:1, although what Dilley would have given me for my cricket is anyone's guess.

My bowling earned me selection for the England Under-19 tour to India before I'd even started at Loughborough, and at university level my batting was maybe 2:2 standard. If I'd studied in the same way I fielded, I probably would have been thrown off the campus but I was gradually gaining experience. The old system, when Oxford and Cambridge were the only university sides to play first class opponents, was being phased out and the MCC were investing a lot of money in centres of excellence at Cardiff, Durham, Leeds and Loughborough. As a result, I was playing with and against a number of players who'd go on to have great careers.

The summer term usually finished around mid-June, at which point I'd go back to Northampton and play for the 2nds. Or at least I would when I wasn't engaged in a personal duel with Mike Hussey in the nets.

I loved Huss. He was seven years older than me and an established, senior professional, but we hit it off immediately because we both loved the game to the extent we'd spend hours staging our own mini-Ashes series in the nets at Wantage Road, well after everyone else had finished. We'd train with everyone else and then concoct scenarios where Huss would need to score so many runs from so many balls from my imaginary field, frequently arguing whether or not my imaginary backward point had caught him.

We used to really live those battles and it drove our coach Nick Cook to distraction. On more than one occasion he'd emerge from a meeting, see we were still out there and yell, 'Guys, go home. It's been two hours!'

I think I made Huss the great player of spin bowling that he became. Whenever I saw him in Test cricket and later in the IPL and watched him sweep and pull the ball for four, I'd think back to those sessions and remember the hours I'd spent watching him get into that exact position. We were like two kids in a playground and we're still friends to this day.

***

Everyone in a county second team either has hopes of breaking into the first team, or of regaining their place if they've been dropped or injured. As a result, the standard was a step up from Minor Counties and university cricket, but nothing can really prepare you for the first time you meet a world-class player at the very height of his powers.

Towards the end of the 2001 season, Northants finally decided to give me my county championship debut against Leicestershire. For the first day I sat and watched as Mister Cricket brutalised Leicestershire's bowlers on his way to 232. On day two, I made a patient 10 from thirty-two balls to help us to 469, but then I had to bowl to Pakistan's Shahid Afridi.

He was the kind of player you needed to get early, because once he had his eye in, he could do serious damage. He took a couple of balls to check me out and then started to launch me, and every other Northants bowler, to every part of the ground. This was four-day cricket and yet he was treating it like a one-dayer, playing Twenty20-style shots before the format had even been invented.

I'd tried every trick I knew against Afridi and nothing had worked. If I took the pace off the ball, he'd spot it. If I sped it up, he'd spot that too. It didn't matter how much it turned, he seemed to know exactly where it was going. Graeme Swann eventually got him for 164, off just 121 balls, but he was the first man out!

You have to be mentally strong to cope with something like that, and I was. I knew that if I kept doing what I was doing, I'd eventually get wickets and the first victim of my first class career was Neil Burns, whom I bowled for 69.

Neil became another lifelong friend. He went on to found the mentoring organisation that would help me out at regular intervals and he now develops leadership programmes for cricket, football and rugby teams. He is very knowledgeable and a great assessor of things.

At the time he was a good county pro, who batted without a grill on his helmet. I got him with a slightly full delivery that he tried to drive. He missed and I hit. That started a mini-collapse. I had Vince Wells caught by Hussey, then Phillip DeFreitas caught by Swanny. They edged into a 15-run lead, but I finished with 4-120 and was quietly elated.

The second innings was the most fun I'd ever had on a cricket field. We'd set them a target of 288 on a disintegrating wicket and they didn't know whether to chase it or block their way to a draw. They went for the latter and were only three down with one session remaining, but then they fell apart. Swanny took 5-34. I bowled as if I was still aiming at the handkerchief I used to aim at as a kid and took 4-11. We'd skittled them for 85 and were mobbed as we walked off.

I felt the same euphoria I'd felt when I'd taken my first wickets as a junior after my dad had press-ganged me into playing. It didn't last.

***

Nothing cures euphoria like a dose of relegation. I wasn't picked for the next match at Kent, but I was recalled for the final game of the season against Somerset at Taunton, well known on the circuit as a bowlers' graveyard.

We needed to win to stay up, but I was struggling to cope with the wind. I forgot the lessons of the onslaught from Afridi and started to panic, rushing the ball through and playing into their hands. I took 2-120 in the first innings and one of my victims was Mark Lathwell, whose presence alone was a reminder of just how quickly a career can enter a fatal tailspin.

I remembered watching him during the 1993 Ashes series. England were getting hammered and Lathwell was supposed to be the Messiah. Neil Burns had played with him and he'd said he was a genius. Marcus Trescothick said Lathwell had left him speechless, but he lasted two matches and never played international cricket again.

Lathwell was an early victim of Australia's strategy of 'mental disintegration'. In a scenario that would resonate with my own Ashes career, England were already 2-0 down in the series when he was selected for the third Test at Trent Bridge. When his opening partner Mike Atherton wished him luck and told him the crowd were rooting for him, he replied, 'They won't be in a minute when I'm on my way back.'

That sense of pessimism defined his career before he'd even faced a ball. When he was dropped everyone said it'd be a matter of time before he was recalled, but he never was. He'd already retired once by the time I played against him.

I could see he was a good player because he made 92 in Somerset's first innings before I finally got him, caught by Paul Taylor. In the second innings I bowled him for 14, and that was the end of his first class career. At the age of twenty-nine, he'd stopped enjoying cricket, so he just gave up.

It would be a long time before I could understand why. I'd had a bad game, we'd lost by four wickets and were dropping down to division two, but the idea of giving up cricket wasn't something I could get my head around.

Chapter 8

Kepler is from Mars, Swanny is from Venus

After the initial excitement of seeing my name on Ceefax – something that sent a wave of excitement around the clubhouse at Luton Town & Indians – my county career took a while to get going, as I juggled my studies with representative games and Loughborough University matches.

I took eleven wickets from two games in 2001, fifteen from five in 2002, eleven from five in 2003 and nought from nought in 2004.

Yet just as my progress towards the ultimate goal of being The Greatest Spin Bowler in the World seemed to be stalling, I was aided by a personality clash between the new Northants coach, Kepler Wessels, and Graeme Swann.

When I'd signed for Northants they'd made it clear I was the number four spinner, behind Swanny, Jason Brown and Michael Davies. Jason was developing well but Michael was released at the end of the 2000 season. Swanny, meanwhile, was still wearing the wounds of the England tour to South Africa from 1999–2000, and when Kepler arrived in 2003, it was obvious from the start that they were opposites who didn't attract. In fact, it'd actually be quite difficult to think of two more contrasting personalities in the history of the game. Swanny was like the schoolchild who desperately wanted to make his mates laugh all the time. He was a really funny guy, but he had a relentless, piss-taking and very English style of humour, which you had to know how to take. Referring to his new boss as 'Kiplur Vissuls' in a dodgy Afrikaans accent probably didn't help.

Kepler was born and raised in apartheid South Africa, although even he wasn't white enough for some of the people he used to play against. He was an Afrikaner and when he was growing up cricket was still seen as 'the Englishman's game', so he was abused by his opponents because his ancestors had been on the other side during the Boer War.

After that he went on to Australian grade cricket, which probably came as something of a relief, given that Aussie cricketers at least liked to sprinkle their abuse with a bit of humour. The problem was, Kepler didn't really do humour. When he was at Northants he tried to ban it from the

Northamptonshire dressing room. As a younger man, however, his way of coping with people who took the piss out of him was to fight them. The Australians admired that and ended up picking him for the national team, but he was never really accepted as a Fair Dinkum Aussie. He was even snubbed by the prime minister, Malcolm Fraser, at a cocktail reception, so it wasn't a huge surprise when he chose to play for South Africa when they were readmitted to international cricket in 1991, although the outraged reaction he got from some of the same Australians who'd shunned him showed he couldn't really win either way.

He was appointed South Africa's first captain of the post-apartheid era, but in his final season he started to have his suspicions that the man groomed to succeed him, Hansie Cronje, was trying to fix matches. I was just starting at Northants when the news broke that the golden boy of South African cricket was a crook and we had trouble believing the news. It was like going to the periodic table and finding a new element had been discovered. We were just going, 'Oh God, this stuff actually exists?'

It was a huge shock and Kepler must have felt betrayed, but he never talked about it. Thus his entire career was played out in the face of constant abuse and adversity. Then he met Swanny, whose idea of adversity was losing to his brother at Top Trumps.

Swanny couldn't help himself at times. When he was selected for the Academy tour to Australia in 2001, it was widely seen as a second chance for players like himself, Rob Key and Andrew Flintoff, who were talented but had a question mark next to their names whenever they were discussed by the selectors.

Swanny barely got out of the airport before he'd C-bombed Rodney Marsh! A member of the support staff had offered to get the new arrivals tickets for a Robbie Williams concert the following week. Marsh asked, 'Who the fuck is Robbie Williams?' and Swanny thought this would be a good moment to imitate his Australian accent and say: 'He's a fucking singer, you ignorant c***!' His tour went downhill from there.

Three years later, he was playing well enough to get recalled to the Academy. He was presumably hoping Marsh had forgotten all about it, only for him to say: 'I am not a man to hold a grudge. Even against someone who calls me an ignorant c***!'

They both laughed, because Marsh could see the funny side of it. By then, however, Swanny had joined Notts, because Kepler had struggled to see the funny side of Graeme Swann, his jokes and his range of comedy accents. Kepler was like an old school headmaster and he saw Swanny's humour was eroding his power in the dressing room. So he told us not to laugh at his jokes and because he was the boss, we had to comply.

Swanny and I only actually played together seven times for Northants. By the time he left he was getting upset about the number of Kolpak players getting in the side, but at the time my attitude was that I needed to improve if I wanted to get selected ahead of them. And as much as I liked Swanny, I also liked Kepler. He was very precise and prescriptive, and his coaching style was very much like commanding an army regiment. It worked for me, but it didn't for players like Swanny who wanted the freedom to express themselves.

I respected his advice and also the fact that he was prepared to listen if I didn't agree with him. A 'well done' from Kepler meant more than it did from other people because he was a man who didn't waste his emotions. You knew you'd earned it. Although when he said it, it sounded more like 'will dunn' because his accent was still so strong.

In 2005, with Swanny having escaped to Nottinghamshire, I made my breakthrough. I'd finally completed my degree and for the first time I was able to concentrate fully on my cricket during the second half of that season. I still only played eight times, but I felt liberated and finished with forty-six wickets at 21.54, the third highest total in Division Two and the best average.

It was a surreal summer because we were playing while the Ashes series was taking place and every now and again the crowd at Wantage Road would erupt when I was midway through my run-up! Northants fans were so loyal that some of them couldn't bear to miss a ball, but almost everyone was either listening to the commentary or checking their phones for updates. If a wicket went down we knew about it, and when we weren't playing we'd have the action on the dressing room TV.

What I didn't realise at the time was how close I'd been to getting called up for England's tour to Pakistan that winter. I'd actually approached Geoff Miller after one match and asked him what I needed to do to get picked. 'Keep taking wickets and David Graveney and I will have to take notice,' was his reply.

The name David Graveney should have stuck in my mind. It didn't. I should also have realised that if I was that close to an England call-up, my punctuality needed to improve. It didn't.

For no obvious reason, I was half an hour late for the final county championship game with Yorkshire that summer. When I got to the dressing room, I was absolutely bricking myself because I was convinced the least Kepler was going to do was punch me. I didn't want to imagine the worst. He was a seriously hard man, who was still boxing into his sixties and had a black belt in karate. There was no point in trying to bullshit him and there was no excuse – short of serious injury or death – that he was going to deem valid. Even the latter probably wouldn't have cut any ice. All I could do was stammer an apology: 'I'm really, really sorry.'

He looked at me for a moment and said, 'Jast go aut and win me the gyme.'

That was a stay of execution. 'OK,' I thought, 'I'd better win it for him.' So I took 5-32 in the first innings, then I made 25 not out with the bat. In the second innings I skittled their top order and ended up with 5-96, helping us to a victory by an innings and 21 runs. Even that wasn't guaranteed to get me out of the doghouse, but when I saw him he just said, 'Will dunn. Bat daunt ivur be lite again!'

So Kepler was like an old school housemaster, but he was the kind of headmaster you started out fearing and grew to respect and eventually admire.

Chapter 9

'It's David Graveney.'
'Sorry, Who are You Again?'

The Pakistan Tour at the end of 2005 was like an ice bath for English cricket, an instant reality check after the Ashes. We lost the three-Test series 2-0 and the one-dayers 3-2.

Of the spinners who made the trip, Ashley Giles was struggling with the hip injury that would eventually end his career. Shaun Udal did OK but he was already in his late thirties. Ian Blackwell took a modest four wickets in the five one-day matches and after some iffy shot-selection one reporter had damned him with the expression 'The stairs don't go all the way up to the loft.' The 'learner' slot that I'd been close to went to Alex Loudon, who only played in the tour matches.

Loudon was another player who struggled with his status as English cricket's next big thing. He was tipped as the natural successor to Ashley Giles, but he was even younger than Mark Lathwell when he retired in 2007. At the age of twenty-seven, Loudon gave it all up to concentrate on his business career and he was arguably more famous for going out with Pippa Middleton than for anything he did as a cricketer.

If I'd been paying closer attention I might have realised I was due for a call-up, but I'd gone to a Nanaksar farm in Edmonton. That was a defining trip in my life, because it reaffirmed my faith as a Sikh and convinced me I was following the right path, although it wasn't exactly a holiday.

Every morning, priests would read from the Guru Granth Sahib, our main religious text, starting at 4 am. They'd teach scripture, chanting and the core principles of Sikhism, one of which is the importance of food. Guru Nanak said that food should be free to all, so feeding the homeless became a vital part of my life, in which I still participate to this day. I spent time harvesting wheat and canola on the farm by the temple and before I left I sought and received my guru's blessing to continue pursuing a career in cricket. It's not an accident that my periods of greatest stability were when I was most in touch with my faith.

From Canada I went to Australia to play grade cricket and it was only when I got back that I realised I might be in with a with a chance of a call-up to the full England side. My phone began humming with messages, because a story had broken on Teletext that I might be in line for selection. I read the article and it included the name 'David Graveney' and the words 'chairman of selectors'. Once again, that name should have stuck in my mind. Once again, it didn't.

***

When I'd got the call to head to the Academy at Loughborough in early 2006, I was obviously pleased, but my expectations were limited to getting selected for the A tour. Loudon and Blackwell were there too and we spent three days going through what I later realised was a trial.

We were in the middle of a touch rugby game on the fourth morning when Peter Moores called me to one side and handed me a telephone. The look on his face should have told me something was up, but he could have arranged for a plane to fly past with a banner trailing the words 'Monty! You're playing for England!', and I still wouldn't have been sure.

'Hello?'

'Is that Monty?'

I didn't recognise the voice. 'Yes?'

'It's David Graveney.'

I didn't recognise the name. Who's David Graveney? I'd genuinely no idea. How could I say that without sounding rude? In the split second I had to think, the best I could come up with was: 'Sorry, who?'

'David Graveney, the chairman of selectors.'

Selectors?

'Congratulations Monty, you're going to India as our sixteenth man.'

'Sorry, who are you again?' I was struggling now.

'David Graveney, the chairman of selectors. We've picked you for the tour to India.'

'What tour to India?' It slowly sank in that I might actually have been talking to the most important man in English cricket, a man who had the power to alter my life forever. And I'd just told him I didn't know who he was. It wasn't on the same level as Swanny C-bombing Rodney Marsh, but even so ...

'The England first team Monty! Congratulations, it's a great achievement for you. Now as I'm sure you're aware, Ashley Giles is injured, so our plan is to use you as back-up to Shaun Udal and Ian Blackwell, and we're likely to be going with two spinners, so you'll have to be ready to come into the team at any time ...'

My head started to reel.

I want to be The Greatest Spin Bowler in the World.
I want to be The Greatest Spin Bowler in the World.
I want to be The Greatest Spin Bowler in the World.

David Graveney keeps talking, but none of it is going in. I think I've just been selected for England. But can he drop me for not knowing who he is? No, because if we was going to drop me he wouldn't be telling me I need to keep it all under my hat, but that I can tell my family and some close friends.

So I can still be The Greatest Spin Bowler in the World?

Eventually I mumbled something and the call ended. I walked back over to the training pitch where the touch rugby game had stopped and Moorsey had clearly told everyone because I was mobbed. Everyone was grinning, shaking my hand, patting me on the back.

They weren't faking it either; there was no jealousy. This was genuine. They were thrilled for me and I realised I should be thrilled for me too. I rang my family.

David later told me he'd never had a call like it. People had laughed, cried with joy and fallen into shock. That was when he was delivering good news. When it was bad news he'd get disappointment, silence and occasionally industrial-strength verbal abuse, but they had all at least known who he was and why he was calling.

Chapter 10

The Last Person You'd Think it Could Happen to …

The India tour changed my life beyond recognition. When I left England I was almost completely unknown, although I wasn't completely unprepared. I'd been to India on several family holidays and on the Under-19 tour I'd been singled out for attention by the media because of my Indian roots, but it was still a culture shock, in more than one sense.

My name had become familiar to the few thousand diehards who followed the county circuit and a few thousand more who watched on Ceefax, but I could still walk around Luton or Northampton and no one would recognise me. By the time I came home, 'Monty Mania' had begun and people were wearing masks with my face on.

I loved everything about being an England cricketer but taking delivery of a special box from the ECB was a particular thrill. It had all the clothing I'd need for the tour in it – the white shirt, the flannels, the sleeveless sweaters, the training tops, the gloves, helmet, pads … It smelt fresh, clean and brand new, and this was barely five years since I'd been carrying my kit around in a plastic bag.

I also loved meeting players I'd been watching on TV just a few months earlier and I particularly loved Andrew Flintoff. When the squad got together at Loughborough before the tour he turned up wearing a Manchester City shirt, shook my hand and said, 'Hello, mate, it's good to meet you. Are you all right?'

He had me at 'Hello mate'.

All right? I'm mates with Andrew Flintoff! Yeah, I'm all right.

***

Freddie would later admit he struggled with depression at times during his career. He was possibly the second to last person on earth you'd suspect of struggling with mental health issues. The very last person you'd think something like that would happen to was Marcus Trescothick, but that, I would later learn, was precisely the point.

Everyone on the circuit looked up to Marcus because he just didn't seem to have any weaknesses. There was an aura about him. Youngsters would go, 'Oh my God, that's Marcus Trescothick,' when he walked past, and I thought he was like a left-handed version of Graham Gooch. When the going got tough, he got tougher, and he was a great person to have on the team. His slip fielding was brilliant and he was always someone you could go to for advice.

There was no sign at all that anything was wrong with him physically. I can remember bowling to him in the nets and he was sweeping me so easily, he might have been swatting away flies. Marcus being Marcus, however, he managed to do it in a way that wouldn't harm my confidence. He'd cream me through square leg, smile and say, 'Try varying the flight a bit more.'

We had absolutely no idea of what he was going through, but the problems had apparently started on the Pakistan tour. His wife had been suffering from post-natal depression and he was already feeling guilty about leaving her in Taunton when he went on a visit to Rawalpindi, which had just been hit by an earthquake.

The idea was sound enough. Michael Vaughan, Matthew Hoggard, Ashley Giles and Marcus were there as guests of the Pakistan Institute of Medical Science. The idea was that the visit would raise awareness of the human catastrophe that was unfolding there.

In Marcus's case, however, it poleaxed him. He saw things he couldn't forget. Children had been maimed by the quake, including a baby he saw with its legs reduced to stumps. The doctors told him their supplies were going to run out in a week and they didn't know how they were going to cope.

This demonstrates another of the myths surrounding mental illness. Well-meaning people will ask you what you have to be depressed about when you are, for example, a well-paid international cricketer as opposed to a beggar. In Marcus's case, it was empathy. He was human. He saw fellow humans suffering and it was too much for him.

It got even worse when he learned his father-in-law had suffered a serious injury after falling off a ladder. His wife begged him to come home, but Michael Vaughan, who can't have known just how bad he was, convinced him to stay. He did, but he was carrying the guilt all the way into the India tour, barely two months later.

When we got to Vadodara for the second tour match, the bus journey from the hotel to the ground took us past dozens of street beggars. We were specifically told not to give them money because they were supposedly controlled by criminal gangs, but Marcus couldn't stop looking at them.

When he saw the beggars holding up their children, it reminded him of his daughter and he started crying in his seat.

We only found this out when his book came out a couple of years later. He hid his tears on the bus, regained his composure and captained us against the President's XI because by then, Vaughan's knee had gone.

Marcus held it together for long enough to bat twice, but after he was out in the second innings he went back to the dressing room and broke down. He was crying his eyes out and gasping for breath. He desperately wanted to go outside but Duncan Fletcher knew what would happen if the public, or worse, the press saw him in that condition so he grabbed him to protect his privacy.

Vaughan ushered us into the next room and we sat there in almost total silence for what seemed like a very long time. After a while, Vaughan mentioned Marcus had once said he'd had to go back to his car so he could 'write something in his book', but he hadn't thought a lot more of it. The truth was that absolutely none of us saw it coming. Sometime later, I saw Marcus at Lord's for a benefit game and it was almost haunting. He just looked at me as if to say, 'I'm not the man you thought I was.'

The human reaction when you see someone suffering like this is to try to help. I can remember telling him he was going to play 150 Tests because I thought that was what he needed to hear, but at that point I didn't understand his illness. I still didn't understand it two years later, when he published his autobiography and said the depression was so bad that he thought he was going to die. It was shocking, but by going public he made it possible for Michael Yardy to get help when he broke down a couple of years later. Matthew Hoggard, Andrew Flintoff and Jonathan Trott all followed suit.

The PCA recognised the dangers and produced a leaflet, which they distributed to all their members, instructing them on what they needed to do if they thought they might be struggling with mental illness.

I should have realised that if someone like Marcus could be struck down in his prime, something like that could easily happen to me. I didn't. I threw my leaflet in the bin.

Chapter 11

Ridiculous to Sublime

The cover story was put out that Marcus had a virus, but that didn't really ring true. He'd been quarantined for a couple of days after picking up a stomach bug, but I'd had the same virus and even though it wasn't pleasant, I'd been dosed up with antibiotics and had managed to struggle through the tour match, taking a wicket in each innings.

The press corps was full of ex-players, most of whom had endured a dose of 'Delhi belly' on previous tours to India, and they all knew that whilst it could banjax you for a couple of days, you were usually better after forty-eight hours.

As that story slowly fell apart, the media team cited additional 'personal reasons' for his departure, which had the advantage of being true, but was still a bit ambiguous and unfortunately created a vacuum. You couldn't really blame them. They'd never had to deal with a situation like this before and almost as soon as Marcus had gone, Michael Vaughan had to follow when it became obvious his knee wasn't going to recover.

Simon Jones was the next player to leave. His departure wasn't such a surprise as he'd always had problems with injuries, but it added to the general air of chaos. Freddie agreed to step up as captain, even though he was in two minds about whether to go home because his wife was about to give birth. He later said he regretted that decision, but his wife gave birth to a healthy boy and he hadn't felt he could turn down the opportunity. He possibly thought he'd be letting the team down if he'd gone given that we were already missing so many senior players, but I think everyone would have understood, even if he wasn't the kind of player you could easily replace.

It was Freddie who told me I'd be making my debut, the night before the first Test, when we were in the team hotel in Nagpur. I waited for the meeting to end, rang my parents and then went to his room, where I showed him all the field placings I'd written down on my hotel notepad, with my detailed plans for every individual batsman. He looked a bit nonplussed, although in his book he later wrote he thought this was 'brilliant' and that he loved my enthusiasm. Even if he had been nonplussed, he was too polite to say so. Flintoff was another brilliant human being.

***

One of the urban myths about my Test career is that I had a premonition that I was going to take Sachin Tendulkar's wicket on my debut. It was a good story, which had one major flaw: it was totally untrue.

I didn't have premonitions. I had visions of grinning Indian batsmen haunting me as I tried to get to sleep and that wasn't exactly the same thing. I had a plan for Sachin, just as I had a plan for every other Indian batsman, but because it was Sachin, I knew the chances of it actually working weren't as high as they would have been if I'd been bowling to someone who wasn't the greatest batsman who'd ever lived.

As we'd won the toss and chosen to bat, I didn't see any action until the morning of the second day, when we were 327-9 and Paul Collingwood was on 79.

The comedian Miles Jupp, who'd blagged his way into the press box claiming he was working for BBC Scotland, later wrote a book called *Fibber in the Heat*, in which he described my Test bow like this: 'The Indian crowd weren't just excited to see Monty arrive at the crease because of his heritage, but also because of his far-reaching reputation as a batsman of unparalleled woefulness.'

I hadn't even faced a ball and my technique was being monstered by Archie the Inventor from Balamory!

Jupp said watching me walk out to bat was like watching a chat show host introduce Johnny Rotten or Crispin Glover: you knew that what followed wasn't going to be good, but it wasn't going to be boring either.

And it wasn't. I got a brilliant reception from the Indian supporters and stayed with Colly for over an hour. He calmed my nerves, gave me advice when he thought I needed it and milked the strike. Eventually he got his ton, although I had to survive two big appeals from Anil Kumble when he was on 93. That was his cue to hit out, as he must have realised I wasn't going to hang around forever, but I lasted for forty-two balls before I was lbw to Sreesanth (who, for the record, was later banned for life for spot-fixing in the IPL).

Colly made 134 and together we put on a stand of 66 for the last wicket. That proved I was a lot better than the rabbit I was reported to be and I was elated I'd been there to help him get past three figures, the first century of an outstanding Test career.

India were 36-1 when I came on to bowl the fifteenth over of their innings, with Wasim Jaffer and Rahul Dravid batting just before tea. Wasim was facing and I had a slip, short leg and silly point in place. I bowled from round the stumps, tossed it up and saw him drive it mid-off for no run. Two dot balls followed, then I got one to turn square in the rough and clip his pad. It went for four byes but it was a moral victory.

The next ball hit him on the pad and we appealed for lbw, but he was saved by his long stride forwards. The sixth ball was a dot. My Test career had started with a maiden over, which helped me relax, but they survived until bad light stopped play, leaving me on 10-3-30-0 at the end of my first day as a Test bowler.

Things livened up the following morning: Hoggy had Dravid lbw in the fifty-first over, then removed Jaffer and VVS Laxman from successive balls in the fifty-third. That brought Tendulkar in and I was temporarily hit by nerves. I had to remind myself I was there on merit and that I had a job to do.

At first I didn't really trouble him. He seemed to be picking me easily, but our plan was to stifle him. He'd been out there for eighty-four minutes and had made just 16 when I had him lbw. He got half-forward and the ball carried straight on into his pads. Aleem Dar put his hand up almost immediately.

Even now people ask me if the celebration was premeditated. Did it look pre-meditated? If it had been pre-meditated I'd have pretended to be James Bond smoking an imaginary cigar, or maybe I'd have acted like Del Boy, playing it 'nice and cool' before falling through the bar.

The ECB's media training only went so far. There was no module entitled 'What to do when you get your hero out'. It wasn't a premeditated celebration, because it didn't occur to me that I might get him out! That's why I started sprinting and high-fiving everyone in my path. We ended up near third man.

I followed that up by bowling Mohammed Kaif, whom I'd first seen in the Under-15 final at Lord's all those years ago. It might have been an even better delivery. It drifted in, hit the pitch and turned past his defensive prod before bending back his off stump. Ian Botham said it was 'magnificent' and I'm told it sent a murmur of excitement through the press box. People who knew their cricket realised England had found a bowler who could trouble the world's best batsmen. In the second innings, I bowled Rahul Dravid but the game ended in a draw and my international career started in a similar manner to my county career – with an initial burst of euphoria followed by a quick reality check.

We lost the second Test in Mohali by nine wickets. I took 1-113 and made a pair, lasting six balls in total, in front of my parents and a few of our closest relatives. No more than seventy of them. I might have had Dravid out twice in the second innings but Andrew Strauss dropped him at slip and then I missed an awkward chance to get him caught and bowled.

I was annoyed with myself, but I didn't think I could be annoyed with Straussy because I knew in the world fielding rankings I was somewhere between Devon Malcolm and Phil Tufnell. What I didn't realise was that in the third Test in Mumbai, I was about to make Phil Tufnell look like Jonty Rhodes.

This was the 'Ring of Fire' Test, when we sang the Johnny Cash song in the dressing room.

'Time for a bit of Johnny Cash, lads!'

Who's Johnny Cash? I literally had no idea, but the horns would kick in and Freddie would start singing like an Elvis impersonator.

'Love, is a burning thing ... and it makes, a fiery ring ...'

We all joined in the chorus: 'and it burns, burns, BURNS! Like a ring of FIRE!'

Nice song. Nice tune. I wasn't sure what it had to do with cricket, or England, but I sang along and after a while I made the connection between the lyrics and the ordeal half the squad had been through shortly after we'd first arrived in India ...

***

I made 3 not out in the first innings and took 1-53 when India batted, getting Anil Kumble lbw. In our second innings I was stranded on 0 not out and I only bowled four overs when they were chasing.

At lunch on the final day we were favourites, but the game was still in the balance, with India on 75-3 and Tendulkar and Dravid at the crease. This was the moment when Vaughany would have given one of his quiet but determined motivational speeches, about creating pressure, taking chances and being 'proper pissed off' if we didn't give it a real go.

Freddie, on the other hand, had a low boredom threshold when it came to motivational speaking and by the end of a three-Test series he was running out of things to say.

So he didn't say anything. He went for a shower, came out stark bollock-naked and let Johnny Cash do the talking for him. Trust me; the sight of Andrew Flintoff dancing around a dressing room without any clothes on isn't something you'll easily forget. We were sitting there killing ourselves with laughter and one by one we started to get up and dance, hammering on the walls, stamping our feet and yelling the chorus at the tops of our voices … 'and it burns, burns, BURNS! Like a ring of FIRE! Like a RING of fiiiire!'

It worked. Even Duncan was apparently stunned by the effect it had, although I suspect he didn't understand why everyone was laughing about the double entendre. Duncan was strictly a single entendre kind of man.

Three balls into the next session, Freddie had Dravid caught behind. It was a beautiful delivery, just short of a length. Dravid, one of the best defensive players in the world, felt he had to go for it and he edged it to Geraint Jones. In the next over, Shaun Udal drew an edge from Tendulkar and he was caught by Ian Bell at short leg. Jimmy Anderson had Virender Sehwag lbw and that brought in MS Dhoni. He edged Jimmy to Owais Shah at first slip, but Owais didn't react in time and the chance went down.

No one remembers this. No one remembers the fact that I took Dhoni eight balls later, with a million-to-one shot from the fourth ball of the forty-fourth over, plucking the ball out of the sun with a catch that cricinfo's ball-by-ball commentator said I'd 'judged to perfection'.

They do, however, remember the first ball of that forty-fourth over, which should, by now, have its own Wikipedia page. It regularly appears in lists of the worst drops of all time and it's inspired a generation of cricket writers. Daniel Bingham said I was spinning like a dog chasing its tail. Miles Jupp, the man who wore a pink kilt on *Balamory*, said it might have been the worst piece of fielding, ever.

Four overs later, the game was over, and in the euphoria of the eventual victory, I was relieved I hadn't cost us the match, but I didn't seriously think anyone was going to forget what had happened.

I wish I'd caught it because that's where the tag came about my fielding. I can remember speaking to Graham Dilley about it when I got back and he basically said to me that if you're fielding in a one-day game or even in a session, you could field well for forty-nine overs, but if you have one bad over, everyone will remember you for it.

That's what ended up happening when I dropped that ball. One minute I'm a hero, the next I'm a zero.

I think the magnitude of it was huge and that set the tone for my fielding from then on. Clumsy mistakes were amplified and if I did make a really big mistake it was like, 'Oh my God, how has he done that?'

And it put a lot of pressure on my fielding. I'm actually not a bad fielder when I put my mind to it, but because of certain mistakes, everyone scrutinised me for it. When you're bowling and you start taking top scalps, everyone thinks you're a world-class bowler. This was the flip side.

***

The Indian fans booed Tendulkar after the defeat. They booed Dravid during the presentation. Their journalists were more worried about Dhoni's 'suicidal' innings than my catching.

And in the post-match press conference an Indian journalist asked, 'Please, Mr Flintoff, what is the significance of the song *Ring of Fire?*'

'It's just a song the boys like,' he said, just about managing to not to laugh.

Chapter 12

Monty Mania

'Monty Mania' apparently started after I'd taken Sachin's wicket in the first Test, although I'd had no idea what was going on back in England until John Etheridge of *The Sun* told me during a press conference.

That was before the Dhoni drop. Freddie had told me interest was building and I was getting a lot of attention from Indian fans, although that wasn't that unusual. Everyone got attention from the Indian fans.

When I got home I realised people were looking at me whenever I went out. They wanted autographs and pictures and I enjoyed it. I did a documentary about my faith with the BBC, I was invited on *Soccer AM* as a celebrity Luton fan (a few years later, I'd go back as a celebrity Arsenal fan) and I was booked to go on *A Question of Sport*, which I used to watch as a kid.

So here's a quick multiple choice question. Which career-defining moment did they use for my introduction?

Was it:

a) the Tendulkar lbw?

b) the ball that bowled Kaif?

c) the Dhoni drop?

Yes, you've guessed it.

I laughed along with the audience, partly because by then I could see the funny side of it but partly because I had to. What was the alternative? If I'd thrown a strop I'd have developed a reputation for being a diva, or worse.

I was at a delicate stage in my mission to become The Greatest Spin Bowler in the World. In six innings, I'd taken five wickets for 312 runs. Getting Tendulkar and Dravid twice proved I had potential, but that was in danger of being eclipsed by my batting, and even more so by my fielding.

I definitely didn't want to be The Worst Fielder in the World so I tried to do something about it. I have huge hands, so why can't I catch? I went back to the Academy, worked on my fitness, worked on my co-ordination, and did specific drills designed to improve my positioning and catching.

The results were … mixed. Duncan thought Udal had outbowled me in India and wanted to stick with him, but his other selectors outvoted him, so he was stuck with me. I kept my place for the Sri Lanka series and the first Test at Lord's was where the full force of Monty Mania really began to hit home. I didn't even bowl in their first innings, but whenever I chased the ball I was getting cheered. It seemed genuine but there was always the worry it might turn into jeering. Any time the ball came near me, people started going 'Whoooooooooooooaaaaaaah!' At one point, Matthew Hoggard said he wasn't sure if they were backing me or putting me under pressure. I thought it was probably both.

Hoggy at least forgave me for dropping catches because I helped him out in awkward social situations, which in Hoggy's case meant almost anywhere where he might have to make polite conversation to a non-cricketer. Or, in fact, anyone other than members of his immediate family and his dogs.

As a teammate he was brilliant – a consistent, loyal and underrated bowler without whom we couldn't have won the Ashes – but he was the sort of person who found socialising an ordeal. Hoggy would rather spend three days bowling at Brian Lara in 35-degree heat than attend a networking buffet.

Unfortunately for him, as England cricketers we're contractually obliged to attend sponsor events. The drill isn't difficult: you turn up, you smile politely, you perfect a laugh you can use when someone cracks a joke that isn't funny but which you nonetheless need to acknowledge, you feign interest in Npower's tariff-switching strategies and it's all over after an hour or two. This is part of the job. This is where you earn your money.

Hoggy knew this but he still couldn't cope with it. It was like asking Phil Tufnell to work on his cover drive. His strategy, when cornered by a sponsor or a dignitary, was to grab me. He'd wheel me over and say, 'Have you met my good friend Monty Panesar?' And then he'd head for the bar.

***

My idea of an awkward social situation was to be fielding at third man when the crowds started singing 'Monty, give us a wave.' I genuinely didn't know how to react. I didn't want to look like I was milking it, but when the crowd ask you to give them a wave you seem arrogant if you don't comply. I was so torn I actually asked the senior players what to do. They told me there was no harm in waving as long as I didn't get distracted, so I did, but it got to the point where they were asking for a wave after every delivery.

I knew that it was harmless, but people were enjoying themselves and there are certain cricket grounds where they look down on that kind of thing. The only guaranteed way to make sure everyone was onside was to take wickets. I took two in the second innings as we drew the first Test at Lord's, then 3–80 in the second Test at Edgbaston, which we won by six wickets. My individual breakthrough came in the third Test at Trent Bridge. By now the fans were coming to games with Monty masks and you'd see white guys in the crowd wearing turbans and false beards.

Once again I was barely used in the first innings, but in the second I took 5–78, including Tharanga and Jayasuriya. I even made 26 in a last wicket stand with Liam Plunkett, but it was overshadowed because we lost heavily and my fielding had once again been an issue.

The worst incident was when I made what I thought was a brilliant diving stop on the boundary, only to see that I'd picked the ball up with one foot still over the rope. The cameras immediately cut to the dressing room balcony, where Duncan Fletcher looked like someone who'd just been told his dog had been run over by a steamroller. If there was no discernible change there, the cameras also showed Matthew Maynard with his hand over his mouth, presumably to stop anyone from lip-reading.

I'd dropped an easy catch at Edgbaston and Duncan had said in the press conference that I needed to improve, but it was a statement of the obvious and he wasn't, at that point, saying anything he hadn't already told me in private. He knew I was trying. He also knew I really didn't want to be the fielding equivalent of Eddie Edwards or Eric the Eel. I just couldn't help it. And I couldn't help the fact that people seemed to love me for it. I hadn't asked anyone to turn up in a mask or a beard, they just did. It was something I was just going to have to get used to. There are, after all, worse things that can happen to a cricketer than being loved, although having said that, Duncan didn't really do love.

Chapter 13

Political Cricket Ball

At first glance, the ECB's guidelines seemed explicit. As England players we were not allowed to be 'political'. The problem for me was that just by walking onto the field I was making a political statement, and it wasn't by choice.

Asians have been playing for England since the nineteenth century but they remain woefully under-represented in almost every major professional sport. In 2015, the editor of *Wisden*, Lawrence Booth, estimated that whilst around 30 to 40 per cent of club cricketers were non-white and predominantly South Asian, only 6 per cent of first class cricketers belonged to the same category.

Booth said: 'At some point, South Asian cricketers are starting to feel that English cricket is not for them. That perception has to change.'

He also pointed out an uncomfortable truth about England's recruitment policies: 'It is perverse to be so reliant on white, Southern Africans and smash–and–grab raids across the Irish Sea, and to ignore the more natural solution on our doorstep.'

In the Irish case the problem was financial rather than political. Cricket had always been a minority sport in Ireland, but by the early 2000s, they were producing some outstanding players like Ed Joyce, Eoin Morgan and Boyd Rankin, all of whom played for England. If I'd been Irish I'd almost certainly have made the same choice given the relative financial awards available, but the flip side is that an emerging cricket nation was weakened.

South Africa was always a more politically loaded subject and the issues dated back to the late sixties when their segregationist, apartheid government refused to select Basil D'Oliveira on the grounds he wasn't white. England offered him the chance to play international cricket but initially left him out of the 1968 tour of his native country, supposedly on cricketing grounds, but in reality because the South African government were going to cancel the tour if England selected a 'coloured' player.

When Tom Cartwright was injured, the cover story was blown. D'Oliveira was called into the squad and the South Africans cancelled the tour. The ICC banned them from playing international cricket and the political fallout is still being felt today.

During the apartheid era, outstanding South African batsmen like Allan Lamb and Robin Smith were controversially drafted into the England side, whilst Kepler Wessels qualified for Australia, even if he was never really accepted as an Aussie. At the same time, cricketers from all over the world, including black and Asian players, were still taking money to play on rebel tours.

When apartheid ended in 1991, South Africa's cricket and rugby teams were still overwhelmingly white and the authorities introduced quotas to encourage players from black, mixed-race and Asian ethnic backgrounds. A consequence of this was that white players who fell on the wrong side of the limits felt as though they were being excluded unfairly; hence Kevin Pietersen's decision to play for England. Even though his mother was English, some people never accepted him. Ten years after he made his debut, Peter Oborne gave him the Tebbit treatment in *The Telegraph*:

> Is it possible to be born and brought up as a South African and give your full loyalty to England? I believe not. Nationality is not just a matter of convenience. It is a matter of identity. Kevin Pietersen may have chosen to come to Britain. But his attitudes and his cast of mind were formed in South Africa. Ultimately, Pietersen has not much idea of what it means to be British.

Ouch. He'd lived here for a decade; I think that must have given him some idea.

It was probably another sign of how attitudes had changed that no one ever questioned whether I should play for England, either here or in India, where the response I got from everyone was overwhelmingly positive. I was the first Sikh to represent the country at any major team sport, not just cricket, and after all the heat they were taking for selecting KP, and to a lesser extent Andrew Strauss (who did, after all, have a nice home counties accent), I think the ECB were delighted I'd broken through.

Cricket could, after all, claim to be well ahead of the other national game.

As of the end of the 2017–18 season, only three British South Asians had played in the English Premier League and only eleven had played in the top four divisions. And as for sports like rugby, athletics and cycling, forget it.

But even with cricket, the numbers still don't add up. Sky's Matt Floyd investigated why relatively few South Asians were turning professional and even at my home club of Luton Town & Indians, he found a number of members supported India or Pakistan.

I can imagine Norman Tebbit reading this and thinking 'Aha!', but Alan Mulally and the Hollioake brothers all grew up in Australia as England supporters. It didn't exempt them from criticism, of course: when Martin McCague, who was born in Northern Ireland but raised in Australia, decided to play for England in 1993, the Aussie press said he was 'the first ever rat to jump aboard a sinking ship'.

But in a free country, what right does anyone have to say who you should support at cricket? Even in countries that aren't free, it's impossible to stop people supporting a team the government doesn't favour (and plenty of dictators have tried).

Nasser Hussain once wrote an article about being in the nets before a Test match and getting wound up by local, British South Asian kids saying Wasim and Waqar were going to kill him. He thought they should have been supporting England, but he also accepted Imran Khan's response: that the route to the top was easier for a public schoolboy with near-white skin like Nasser than it was for an Asian growing up in an urban area like Birmingham, Bradford or Luton.

I didn't encounter overt racism in the game, but unconscious bias was a problem. There's still a perception in the game that West Indians make natural fast bowlers and Asians are all spinners. Then there are the more worrying, sub-conscious associations. During the summer of 2006, while I was making my breakthrough, Hashim Amla, a devout Muslim, was establishing himself as one of South Africa's greatest ever batsmen.

Amla is one of the classiest players ever to pick up a cricket bat, a beautiful technician who also delivers in the hard currency of runs. He averages over 47 in Test cricket and nearly 50 in ODIs. He also has a bald head and a long beard, and early in his career he was written off as a 'quota' player. When he caught Kumar Sangakkara during a game with Sri Lanka, Dean Jones, the former Australia batsman who was commentating, said, 'The terrorist has got another wicket,' live on television.

His employers sacked him immediately and Jones issued an apparently sincere public apology, but when he rang Amla to apologise personally, he said, 'I'm sorry mate, I didn't mean for it to come out on air,' as if saying it when the microphone was off would have somehow made it acceptable.

In Jones's case he probably didn't even realise he was being offensive, yet when an as-yet-unnamed Australian player called Moeen Ali 'Osama' during the 2015 Ashes, he was almost certainly doing it to cause a reaction.

In my entire playing career I never came across anyone who thought that kind of remark was fair game. Something must have gone seriously wrong with the culture of that dressing room. The Australians I played against were merciless piss-takers, but they had a sense of humour as long as they were winning, which they usually were. Even when they weren't, such as in Cardiff, no one ever crossed that line.

If anyone had said anything like that to me, I probably would have just laughed back at them, but I can understand why he was so angry. Play cricket, say other stuff, but you don't have to say stuff like that.

Cricket's a different game to most sports. Players play with and spend so much time with each other that it becomes like a family, or a group of friends. If anything, you might use each other's weaknesses for humour, like your fitness being rubbish, but something to do with mental health or religion is outside of the boundaries of sledging. You don't go beyond that.

***

The only place where I ever get serious abuse is, unsurprisingly, online.

In early 2017, I did an interview with Robbie Lyle from Arsenal Fan TV, a YouTube channel that became a viral sensation because it filmed fans going into meltdown every time the Gunners lost. Or drew. In fact, if Arsenal didn't win by at least five goals against lesser opponents, Arsenal Fan TV would feature at least two fans who'd managed to work themselves into a state of piss-boiling rage.

On the increasingly rare occasions we got a result against one of the bigger sides, teams that we considered to be our natural rivals, Robbie could still find someone with the mental agility to claim that beating Man United or Chelsea was a disaster because it meant Arsene Wenger wouldn't get sacked.

The fan base was in a state of virtual civil war at the time, between the 'Wenger Out' brigade, spearheaded by Piers Morgan and their enemies, the 'AKBs', which stood for 'Arsene Knows Best'.

It was poisonous. People were nearly fighting each other in the stadium but because fans from rival clubs thought it was hysterical, Arsenal Fan TV got better viewing figures than some of the actual matches.

After a match Robbie would ask a fan, 'How is it we just crumble like this?'

And a guy with a pierced nose and a bandana would say, 'Because we are shit!'

A lot of Arsenal fans couldn't bear to watch and people would chant 'Fucking embarrassing' at Robbie when he was trying to film, but he is a genuine fan.

I thought he was a nice guy and I was happy to give him an interview. We had a nice chat and when he asked me about Wenger, I was honest: I loved the man and I always had. I also knew from my studies just what a genius he was, so I said he should be given more time and even said I was going to post a blog called '*J'adore Arsene Wenger*'.

That went down about as well as a Glasgow Rangers shirt in the Vatican.

There were 684 comments on YouTube and 680 of them were people calling me a 'wanker', a 'fucking moron', an 'idiot' and significantly worse. About 300 of them said I should 'stick to cricket'. Someone said he thought I'd been hit on the head with a cricket ball once too often and another said, 'This is why you're not in the England team,' which seemed like a bit of a leap.

I might have passed the Tebbit test, but in the Wenger test, I got a D minus.

***

Imran's response to Nasser helped him realise we all have to do more to make the England team more attractive to every part of our society.

The ECB, to their credit, have always known that. So while we, as players, were instructed not to be political, I was photographed, with their approval, holding a St George's flag. That kind of symbolism was fine. What they didn't want was me taking five wickets and unveiling a specially printed T-shirt saying 'I've passed the Tebbit test' during the post-match press conference.

They needn't have worried about me personally (I'd signed a contract and I didn't fancy the fine) but I couldn't control what other people wrote about me.

During that same summer, as Monty Mania started to kick in, a reporter from *The Independent* called Matthew Beard went to Luton Town & Indians, where my brother Isher was playing. Beard had an agenda and the clumsiness of the questioning was embarrassing: 'Luton is associated with Muslim extremism: what can Monty do to change that?'

Isher was only nineteen at the time and Beard said he 'seemed irritated' by the question. Imagine that! What was he supposed to say? 'White guys started two world wars: what can you do to change that?' 'Do people associate you with extremism because your name is Beard?' And, 'Can't you tell the difference between a Sikh and a Muslim?'

The problem was there were still a lot of people who couldn't, and in hindsight I can see what *The Independent* were trying to do. Islamophobia was increasing and this was an attempt to push back against it, even if it meant rallying behind an English Sikh cricketer. The article made a reference to the Tebbit test and reported that the Muslim and Sikh kids were all supporting England.

I was twenty-three and it was too much to get my head around. Politics fascinates me now, but at the time I couldn't afford to think about it. I wanted to be The Greatest Spin Bowler in the World and after the summer of 2006, I was tantalisingly close.

Chapter 14

No Sandpaper was used in the Making of this Test Series

I took seventeen wickets in the Pakistan series and the heat around my fielding was dying down, although that was mainly because the media had a bigger story to get their teeth into, when the ball-tampering saga re-ignited.

The weird thing about a cricket scandal is that you can be right in the eye of the storm and still know absolutely nothing about what's going on.

By the time we got to The Oval we were 2-0 up after three Tests and I'd already taken sixteen wickets, including 5-72 in the second innings at Old Trafford. My list of victims was also getting more impressive. To Tendulkar and Dravid you could add Sangakkara (twice) and Jayasuriya from the Sri Lanka series, plus Younis Khan, Mohammad Yousuf and Inzamam.

We were, however, struggling in the fourth Test. At tea on day four we were four wickets down in our second innings and still 33 runs behind. At which point, an international incident broke out in the next room. At the end of the fifty-sixth over, the umpires, Darrell Hair and Billy Doctrove, had started looking at the state of the ball. They asked for a replacement box to be sent out and selected a new one. That wasn't that unusual, but Hair then started tapping his shoulder.

It looked like some kind of Masonic gesture and I didn't know what it meant, so I asked around the dressing room and realised no one else knew either. The TV was on, but muted, so we turned the sound up and found out at the same time everyone else did. Five penalty runs, awarded in accordance with rule 42.3.

Even then, we didn't have any idea just how angry Pakistan were.

Inzamam looked angry, but that was just normal. Bob Woolmer was seen heading to the match referee's office with a copy of the rule book under his arm and the bowlers looked upset, but we put that down to the way KP and Paul Collingwood were smashing them round the park. They celebrated as usual when they got KP for 96 and the teams came off early for bad light at 3.45 pm.

We had an extended tea interval while the light improved and the umpires were back out in the middle just under an hour later. Colly and Belly were stood in the corridor, waiting for Pakistan to come out, but nothing happened. They must have spent the entire interval smouldering. The crowd started a slow handclap in protest and a Mexican wave broke out, which is seldom a good sign. Belly and Colly went out to join the umpires in the middle, but Kamran Akmal walked out onto the balcony and started reading a paper!

By now we'd worked out they were protesting about the 'insult' of the 5-run penalty. When Umpire Hair took the bails off, that technically meant we'd won the game by forfeit, but no one seriously thought the match would be abandoned.

Pakistan went back out. We stayed put. The umpires stayed put.

Pakistan came back in and Shahryar Khan of the PCB went out to speak to Mark Nicholas, claiming they were 'deeply insulted and deeply aggrieved about the slur of ball tampering', but that they were prepared and indeed 'eager' to play on. When Khan then started saying it was a slur on Pakistan's cricketing establishment and the entire nation however, I got the feeling it wasn't going to end well.

Khan's outrage was directed entirely at the umpires and he claimed the relationship between the two sides was 'excellent'. That might have been stretching things. I got on well with the Pakistan boys and I certainly hadn't noticed any animosity during this series, but there was always an undercurrent of tension when they played England. It had been brewing since 1992. Or maybe the Shakoor Rana–Mike Gatting ruckus in 1987. Or maybe even since the partition of 1947.

The subtext was that Pakistan thought England were a bunch of cheats, with an additional accusation of hypocrisy chucked in, given that English cricketers had been accusing Pakistan's cricketers (and umpires) of cheating for at least twenty years. Pakistan were also incensed by a couple of umpiring decisions during the Faisalabad Test in 2005, when Darrell Hair just happened to be one of the umpires.

The England boys were also still simmering about an episode that took place during the same Test. A huge explosion had taken place during the middle of a session and although it eventually turned out to be a gas canister, everyone thought a bomb had gone off and that a terrorist incident was taking place.

Play was halted while they checked to see if everyone was OK, but in the confusion, Shahid Afridi actually started grinding his spikes into the wicket, which eventually got him a ban. The fact he could do that while everyone was worrying if someone had been killed had seriously pissed off the England boys. Even Marcus Trescothick, The Nicest Man in the World, said he was unimpressed, so the rest of the dressing room must have been steaming.

If one incident could sum up the chaos of the way cricket is governed, this was it. At 5.30 pm, when Pakistan came back in for what turned out to be the final time, the ground was still packed, because no one had bothered to tell the supporters what was going on. That was because no one knew. We didn't know.

If an alien spacecraft had landed on the square at that point and a little green man had said 'Take me to your leader,' everyone would just have started looking at each other.

We sat there watching the TV. Atherton was laying into Darrell Hair. Nasser was laying into the ICC. An announcement was made that there would be no further play that evening, so all the fans started filing out, but we were still suffering death by a thousand meetings.

The ICC were talking to the ECB and the PCB, and the Chief Executive of The Oval was involved, as were the captains, the match referee and the umpires. In one of the meetings, Hair apparently lost his rag when Inzamam demanded to know why they were being accused. According to Duncan, he said, 'You know what was going on out there,' and stormed out. At 10 pm, when some of them had presumably lost the will to live, they decided to call the game off.

The following morning, Pakistan's coach, Bob Woolmer, said all they'd wanted to do was make a protest. He said he'd interviewed every member of the team 'under oath' and they'd all denied cheating. They'd wanted to make their point and then start playing again.

I believed him, and it's one of my lasting regrets that I never got the chance to talk to him properly because he was one of the most intelligent men in the game.

If someone of his stature had been in charge of the ICC, the game would never have been abandoned. He would have got everyone together, had a quiet word with whoever was concerned and we'd have been playing again within twenty minutes. The episode wouldn't have gone unnoticed, but it wouldn't have turned into an intercontinental diplomatic scandal.

Unfortunately he wasn't.

**

I liked and respected Darrell Hair, but the Pakistan boys couldn't be doing with him. They thought he had an officious style and didn't like the way he talked to them. They'd already made a complaint about him after the

Headingley Test. I don't think there was any racial element to it; it was more a question of style. Some of the umpires on the circuit, like Simon Taufel, were happy to engage with the teams, talk to the players and let them know what they expected of them.

Darrell was more in the Kepler Wessels mode: his word was the law. I didn't have a problem with that, because you knew exactly where you stood, but his tone upset people. As far as he was concerned, the moment he'd taken the bails off, that was it: game over. In his case that was the literal truth, because it ended his career.

A few days later, he emailed the ICC and offered to quit if they paid him $500,000. It didn't look good but he argued it was a severance payment to cover his loss of earnings. He withdrew the 'offer' but things got worse for him. The ICC banned him after a two-day meeting and in 2007 he said he was suing them and the PCB for racial discrimination, though he later dropped that case.

Nasim Ashraf, the chairman of the PCB, said the case reflected badly on his 'mental status'. I don't think he was being sympathetic. What if Darrell was suffering from mental health issues? What if he actually needed help? He did return as an international umpire, but only for six months. He went into coaching, but that didn't last and in 2017 he was working in an off licence when he was arrested. He'd become addicted to gambling and just said, 'You got me,' when his employers confronted him. He paid back over $9,000 that he'd stolen and was spared jail provided he agreed to an eighteen-month good behaviour bond.

At the time he was banned from cricket, Darrell was ranked as the number one umpire in the world for decision-making. A decade later, he was a criminal.

A lot of people found his fall from grace funny but by 2017, I was all too aware of how cricket could affect your mental health. For an umpire the game must be even lonelier. I wonder if anyone at the ICC ever thought to ask him how he was actually feeling.

***

Pakistan were officially exonerated of ball-tampering, but that doesn't mean it didn't happen.

By then, Imran Khan had admitted he used to gouge the ball using a bottle top and in his autobiography he claimed he didn't really think ball-tampering was cheating.

We'd all seen Afridi dancing on the wicket in Faisalabad, and in 2010, he actually bit a ball like he was chomping into a toffee apple during a T20 match with Australia.

The laws of cricket say:

> It is an offence for any player to take any action which changes the condition of the ball. Except in carrying out his/her normal duties, a batsman is not allowed to wilfully damage the ball. A fielder may, however, polish the ball on his/her clothing provided that no artificial substance is used and that such polishing wastes no time.

We all tried to change the condition of the ball, because reverse swing has such a huge impact. The rest is open to interpretation.

By the Ashes series of 2005, Freddie and Simon Jones were nearly as clever at reverse swing as Wasim and Waqar had once been. Their biggest victim was Adam Gilchrist, who was the kind of player who could destroy you, physically and mentally, with a counter-attack. Australia could be in trouble at five or six down and Gilly would come in and score a run-a-ball hundred that could psychologically break the opposition. His weakness, however, was that he played in a 45 degree arc. He wasn't as straight as you'd think and when the ball started to reverse swing, he couldn't cope with it.

In the third Test of that series, Simon Jones reverse swung the ball into Michael Clarke's off stump as he was shouldering arms. It was a few seconds of brilliance that had taken hours of preparation, as I'd soon come to learn.

When I came into the side, my job was to prepare the ball for the seamers. They'd say, 'Listen mate, if you want to bowl with us it's on one condition. Make sure you don't get your sweaty hands on our shiny side.'

Jimmy Anderson in particular would say, 'Look Monty, I just want you to keep that ball as dry as possible,' and I became very good at it because if I got it wrong it'd take another five overs to get it right.

Whether we broke the laws or not again depends on how you interpret them. We found that mints and sun cream had an effect on the saliva, and that helped the ball to reverse. I might also have 'accidentally' caught the ball on the zip of my trouser pocket to rough it up a little. That probably was a hairline fracture of the spirit of the game, even if the laws said you were allowed to 'use your uniform'.

We wouldn't have gone any further than that. The ECB was still smarting from 'dirt gate' when Mike Atherton was caught brown-handed with mud in his pockets during a Test with South Africa in 1994. His initial defence to the England management was that he was trying to maintain the condition of the ball rather than alter it, but when he went to the match referee, he said the dirt was to keep his hands dry.

He was fined £2,000 and only just held on to his job.

If Pakistan were ball-tampering, they weren't doing anything that obvious because, believe me, we were watching them. It wasn't because we thought they were cheating; we wanted to know how they were getting it to move so much. When he wasn't batting, Marcus would sit there with his binoculars, tracking the ball to see how they were preparing it. He didn't see any skulduggery and with so many cameras at a Test match, you just wouldn't get away with it. Afridi found that out when he bit the ball in 2010. He apologised and I think everyone probably thought ball-tampering had reached its nadir. We'd obviously underestimated the Australians.

***

Almost everything I know about the end of this Test match is second-hand. I heard about it from watching Sky or reading about it online.

A couple of days after the game was abandoned, I was back on county duty with Northants and our overseas player Chris Rogers was grilling me for the inside story. I couldn't tell him, even though it had happened right under my nose. Maybe I should consider a career in journalism when the cricket ends.

Chapter 15

The Greatest Spin Bowler in the World?
(Part 1)

By the end of the Pakistan series that summer, Duncan was describing me as the best finger spinner in the world and lauding me for my control. Duncan liked control.

As with Kepler Wessels, another intensely serious African coach, it meant more coming from someone like Duncan than it might have done from someone who was always telling you that you were world class when you suspected they were trying to work on your confidence. And when the praise started coming from some genuine legends of the game, that also made me feel like I was close to achieving my target.

Ian Botham wrote a column in *The Mirror* saying I was the finest left-arm spinner in the world and that he'd 'rather write a suicide note than tell the Aussies how to handle Monty's craft and variations'.

I hope you can understand why I'd like to devote just a bit of space to Sir Ian's full remarks:

> For a start, like all world-class spinners, he gives the ball a good rip. Secondly, admire his attacking line, coming round the wicket to the right-hander and pitching the ball around middle and off stumps.

> The batsman has to play almost every ball. At the point of delivery, Panesar stays tall and releases the ball at the highest point of his bowling arm's arc.

> Even some of the best players of spin in the world have not been able to cope with Panesar's drift, bounce and spin. Not only is Monty growing in stature, but he is giving his captain an element of mystery that so many England sides have been lacking for years.

> And the mystery is this – how can a finger-spinner turn the ball so far and yet maintain a disciplined line and length?

How does it feel when a national hero thinks you're the best left-armer in the world? How do you think it feels? It feels great!

When Duncan brought his book out a year later he had a go at Sir Ian, implying the players didn't respect his commentary and that we tried to avoid him in social situations.

The first part wasn't true, or at least it wasn't as far as I was concerned. The second part was true, but it was purely down to self-preservation. Duncan cited an episode when the Hampshire chairman Rob Bransgrove had asked us onto his boat for a party after a game with Canada during the World Cup. KP asked if Botham was going and when Bransgrove said 'Yes', it is true that half a dozen people said 'No thanks', and it is true that we all laughed, but it wasn't because we didn't like him. It was because we were worried we wouldn't get to the next game with our motor functions intact.

***

Duncan might have thought I was the best finger spinner in the world, but that didn't mean he necessarily felt he had to pick me. I suspect he always thought I was keeping the seat warm for Ashley Giles, who, after a year out with injury, was back for the 2006–07 Ashes tour.

Ashley wasn't likely to bowl a side out on his own, but he could nail down an end, create pressure and chip in with the odd wicket, as he had during the 2005 series. As he could bat and, perhaps more crucially, catch, there was a definite logic to his selection for the first Test at the Gabba, but I still thought I had a good chance of playing right up until the moment Freddie read out the eleventh name on the team sheet.

I'd certainly prepared as though I was going to be thrown in at the deep end. Mental disintegration was a collective national effort in Australia. It started at immigration where the border guards would unleash the 'good luck' joke. In the course of the average unsuccessful Ashes tour an England cricketer hears the 'good luck' joke approximately 600 times. Even on a successful tour you'll still probably reach treble figures.

Everyone knows it, from priests, to small children. They say 'good luck!', pause for a couple of seconds and then add, 'You're gonna need it!' There's a stock reply for the border guards. When they ask if you have a criminal record, you say, 'Why, do you still need one?' Although to be honest, in the current climate I wouldn't risk this if you have a beard or a patka.

The 'good luck' joke is obviously intended as humour, but there was a more sinister side to playing in Australia. I was warned that as a Sikh I'd be a target for 'banter'. This was an era when cricketers still got letters, as opposed to several thousand angry social media messages, and a man called Peter Hall who lived in the Wirral wrote to me saying he'd been brought up in Australia but had Eurasian parents. His advice was that if they barracked me it meant they liked me and that as long as I responded in a positive way, I'd win them over.

That was true, up to a point. There were various methods for getting the Australians onside. The first was the Phil Tufnell method. Tuffers has built his after-dinner speaking career around the time a heckler asked him if he could lend him his brain, because he was 'building an idiot'. It was a great line and the heckler gave it to Tuffers free of charge. Tuffers laughed along, memorised it and has been making money out of it ever since.

Then there's the Ronnie Irani method: when he realised that several hundred Aussies were copying his warm-up routine, he milked it for all it was worth and clearly loved every second of it. That was one of cricket's great 'feel-good' moments.

And then there was the Ian Botham method: monster them. Beefy spent the best part of fifteen years beating the Australians and when they tried the old 'How's your wife and my kids?' line on him, he allegedly replied, 'The wife's fine: the kids are all retards.'

I also knew there was a more sinister side to the heckling. Michael Holding had to endure serious racial abuse from Australian crowds as a young bowler and while things had improved since then, the so-called banter was still morphing into something worse.

Graeme Smith said I was 'going to cop an unbelievable amount of abuse'. He'd captained South Africa there the previous year and they'd reported multiple incidents during the tour.

A story got out that I'd had counselling. They were a few years too early on that one. What had actually happened was that the ECB, having learned the lessons of the Mark Lathwell experiment, were starting to understand the value of sports psychology. The entire squad had had a session with Steve Bull on scenarios we were likely to face and how we'd cope with them. Scenarios like how to cope when a newspaper completely fabricates a story about how you need counselling and it gets completely misinterpreted by the world's greatest seam bowler, when all you actually did was attend a sports psychology seminar.

My mental health was fairly robust at that point. When Glenn McGrath said I was 'soft' for having had counselling I hadn't actually had, I just laughed it off. Marcus, however, was struggling again. He'd played in the Test series that summer but he was worried the medication was dulling his reactions. He felt that going to the ICC Champions Trophy in India would jeopardise his recovery and Duncan agreed he should stay at home and prioritise the Ashes, but a news organisation with a reputation for using illegal methods somehow found this out. They were planning to break the story before he was ready and the ECB decided that was the moment they should come clean about what had happened in India.

I don't know if being 'outed' made Marcus's condition worse, but it can't have helped. When we got to Australia he couldn't cope. Marcus had been there before, of course, but that was in 2001–2002, when we'd had the decency to spend fifteen years losing to Australians. They could treat us as a joke. Now, because we'd beaten them in 2005, there was more of an edge to it. Marcus described the reception we got as one of 'unbridled hostility' and he found the hype painful.

The margins in that 2005 series had been wafer-thin. We nearly blew both of the matches we won and whilst we should have won the drawn Test at Old Trafford, we could easily have lost at The Oval as well. In situations like those, Vaughan was the sort of captain who could make a difference by giving you the belief you need to get over the line. He hated defeatism and usually strangled it at birth but this time he wasn't there to stop it from spreading, and it was also obvious we were going to miss his runs.

Under normal circumstances Marcus would have been his natural successor, but due to his issues he wasn't considered. That left Duncan with a straight choice between Freddie and Andrew Strauss. The other selectors were split so he had the casting vote, and he apparently went with Freddie because he'd seen a motivational DVD in which someone had flashed up a caption saying, 'This team has to be together to beat Australia.'

Who knew that a caption could have that much influence?

Duncan admitted in his autobiography that he wasn't sure it was the right call, but that he was worried 'two' of the senior players wouldn't respect Strauss if he was given the job. He didn't name the two players he was worried about, but he didn't really have to because in the next paragraph he said he was worried that Freddie and Harmy would get into trouble if Freddie wasn't made captain. Then again, he also said that before I was called up, Hoggy had used the code PT to describe Strauss and Alex Loudon. PT stood for 'posh twats'.

***

The mental and physical fragility seemed contagious.

During the tour match against New South Wales, Marcus asked the umpire if he could leave the field to go to the toilet. He never came back.

Marcus broke down completely in the dressing room while we were in the field. Game over. He'd been torn about giving up his medication before the tour and subsequently agonised about going back on his pills. Some of the boys who knew him best had seen the warning signs and given what had happened in India, it wasn't a surprise. It was, however, a shock.

When we came off at stumps Duncan said, 'You all know that Tres has gone home. I think we should all spare a thought for him now and remember he has been an absolute legend for England.'

He was using the past tense, as if someone had died. In a way, they had. The Trescothick who'd played for England had gone and he wasn't coming back. You aren't human if you can witness something like that and not be affected by it, even if, like me, you still don't think it'll ever happen to you. Even Duncan, who hardly ever showed emotion, was more affected than he let on. After Marcus's first breakdown in India he'd said he never wanted to see that happen to anyone ever again, but it had, and now it was happening to Steve Harmison as well. He had a reputation for homesickness and as he'd once spent 300 nights of a year away from home, people could understand that. They didn't know he was clinically depressed.

Of the team that had beaten Australia less than eighteen months earlier, Vaughan and Jones were injured, Trescothick had gone home, while Freddie and Harmy had as yet undetected mental health issues that manifested themselves in the kind of behaviour Duncan didn't appreciate.

He was also under pressure to select Chris Read instead of Geraint Jones. He resisted that because he thought Read had technical flaws and he also claimed he wasn't aggressive enough, the same charge he'd make against me. Duncan had made up his mind to go with a single spinner in the first Test. In the tour match against New South Wales he felt Ashley had performed better than I had and as he took three wickets to my one, he had the statistics to back him up.

Mentally, however, I was coping well. Graeme Smith's prediction that I'd be racially abused reportedly came true during the same tour match when a fan was alleged to have yelled that I was a 'stupid Indian who couldn't speak English'. I didn't hear it and it didn't affect me. Even if I had heard it, I doubt I would have batted an eyelid.

The fact this was big news suggested Australia was at least taking its racism problem seriously. The fact that Cricket Australia's Chief Executive James Sutherland said, 'I don't think there's too much racist about that,' suggested that Cricket Australia probably needed to send Sutherland on a course.

KP was getting abuse as well, along the lines that he was a 'fucking South African', but that just fired him up even more.

The Australian players were told not to sledge KP for precisely that reason. To them, sledging was like a branch of science.

***

The alarm bell should perhaps have started ringing when I was picked for the final tour match in Adelaide, along with Chris Read, Liam Plunkett and Saj Mahmood. We were the only Ashes squad players selected for what was billed as an Invitational XI, the others being recently retired legends like Alec Stewart and Robin Smith.

I took 2-63 but it wasn't enough for Duncan. It wasn't much of a consolation to find out he'd been agonising over the decision, to the extent that he seemed to be asking almost every ex-player and pundit on the tour. To be honest, I think he already knew that he was going to pick Ashley, but he wanted reassurance. Apparently almost everyone other than Nasser Hussain told him Ashley should play ahead of me. When Nasser told him he should worry about the repercussions of excluding me if things went wrong, that was apparently what made up his mind.

Duncan hated the idea of selecting the team based on the risk of a public backlash, so Ashley was in and I was out. He was pilloried for it when it backfired but I'm sure he feels that plenty of the people who were raging at him with the benefit of hindsight would have made exactly the same call if they'd been in his shoes. Even I saw the logic of it. Duncan's need for three-dimensional talent went well beyond the cricket field. In 2004, he'd even released England's scorer Malcolm Ashton because he couldn't multi-task.

Ashley averaged over 20 with the bat and he could hang around for a long time if his partner needed support. He knew how to win Test matches against Australia and he'd been there at Trent Bridge when we were collapsing to within three wickets of losing the Ashes, again.

And for me it wasn't personal. I looked up to Ashley, respected him and tried to learn whatever I could from him. None of which could alter the fact that it was still the biggest disappointment of my career when, on the day before the game, Freddie read out the team sheet.

'Four, Collingwood. Five, Pietersen. Six, Flintoff. Seven, Jones. Eight Giles ...'

Shit. Maybe he's playing two spinners?

'Nine, Hoggard. Ten, Harmison. Eleven, Anderson.'

In the Scorsese-directed film of my life this will be the moment where time slows to a crawl. The camera would cut to a close-up of Duncan, his lips moving at a tenth of their normal speed and a distorted sound emerging.

I don't know how long I stayed in this state, but I managed to get together enough to ask him to repeat himself.

'I'm worried about Australia batting first … need insurance … balance …'

I went over to Ashley, shook his hand and wished him luck. It hurt like hell, but I meant it.

And then I went back to my room and stared at the same spot on the ceiling for what might have been a few minutes and what could equally have been several hours.

***

I later found out that Duncan said, 'I've just put my job on the line' to Matthew Maynard and Kevin Shine after giving me the bad news. Just as when he picked Freddie over Strauss for the captain's job, he knew it was the kind of call that had the potential to seriously backfire if things went wrong, and given what had already happened on the tour, he knew there was a strong chance they would.

By contrast, after an evening in the purgatory that all non-playing cricketers visit, I was more like my usual self the following morning. I warmed up as usual, went out for the anthems and then retired to the balcony with Chris Read, the other pacifist in the squad.

Matthew Hoggard usually bowled the first delivery, but Freddie wanted Steve Harmison to get us under way, so he handed him the ball. Harmy immediately gave it back to him. The ball screamed through to Freddie at second slip and into his big, bucket-like hands. The only problem was, Justin Langer hadn't hit it. He wouldn't have been able to reach it.

A lot has been said about this delivery and how it encapsulated what was to follow, but it was just a single ball. It didn't necessarily have to set the tone for what was to follow. It was the 1,200 balls that we bowled after that one that were the problem. As were at least twenty of the 732 that we faced.

We actually played well at times, especially Colly and KP during our second innings, but against an Australian side of that quality, everyone had to be near or at the top of their game if we were to stand a chance.

I watched Mike Hussey make a measured 86 and reflected how much all those hours we'd spent in the nets at Wantage Road, fighting out our own private Ashes battles, had helped him.

We took it to the fifth day, but the final margin of defeat was a crushing 277 runs and the recriminations started well before the end.

It's amazing how you can become a better player by not actually playing. A chorus of pundits said I should have been selected ahead of Ashley, including my old county coach at Northants, Nick Cook. Duncan's response was to blame Cookie for the fact that after several years under his tutelage, I didn't have an arm ball and I couldn't field or bat. It was at that point that I started to question whether Duncan would ever enjoy a post-cricket career as a motivational speaker.

***

The psychological warfare continued. While in Brisbane, I visited a restaurant called Gandhi on Little Stanley Street. A couple of days later, a reporter somehow managed to turn this into a story about me being disloyal to India because Indira Gandhi had been assassinated by a Sikh.

I'm not sure this reporter's stairs went all the way up to the loft. His argument was that I was being disloyal to a country I didn't actually represent, because someone wearing a turban had killed the prime minister of India when I was two years old. And he'd arrived at this conclusion after I'd visited a restaurant named after Mahatma Gandhi, who wasn't actually a relative of Indira but who had also been assassinated, in his case by a Hindu extremist.

I'm not sure where this kind of argument ends.

Do white guys who don't wear headgear ever get blamed for what happened to JFK in Dallas in 1963? Shane Warne is white and he never wears a hat when he's bowling. Lee Harvey Oswald was white and he didn't wear a hat either. Was Warnie somehow being disloyal to the USA, even though he's Australian? If you go to the city of Lincoln and have a beard, are you somehow traducing the memory of Abraham Lincoln? Is it disrespectful to listen to *Take Me Out* by Franz Ferdinand if you're on a city break to Sarajevo?

Maybe the author was the idiot the Bay 13 heckler had built using Phil Tufnell's brain.

Whatever his reasons, it wasn't my problem. Thanks to Steve Bull's sessions, I knew how to deal with this kind of poundshop racism.

It was also completely untypical of the reception I got when I met the Australian public face to face. I might have heard the 'good luck' joke a few hundred times, but it was always delivered with a smile.

Even though they always meant it.

***

With every ball I didn't bowl my stature grew. Duncan had actually wanted me to play in the second Test at Adelaide because he thought we needed to go with two spinners, but on this occasion his fellow selectors outvoted him and he ended up copping the flak for it.

It was the last Test Ashley would ever play. He didn't bat or bowl badly in the first innings but he was one of several scapegoats for our second innings collapse.

I can't honestly say if I'd have bowled any better than him but he also dropped Ricky Ponting when he was on 35, and although he was usually an excellent fielder, it was the kind of chance even I might have taken. Ricky made another 107 runs.

There's no good way to lose a game of cricket but this has to be one of the worst. It was the equivalent of the 1999 European Cup final, when Bayern Munich were the better team for ninety minutes and still lost. We were the better side for four days. So what? Do you get a gold medal for leading the Olympic marathon after 25 miles?

It was bad enough watching from the balcony, unable to do anything. The only mitigation was that we were watching The Greatest Spin Bowler in the World go about his business. That was where I needed to be. Shane Warne was maybe the greatest cricketer that ever lived, let alone the greatest bowler.

We went from 69-2 to 129 all out, and with every wicket that fell there was the creeping realisation that a game that had seemed dead was not only reviving, it was drifting away from us.

It was a defeat that left permanent scars on some of our team, and I think Duncan as well. Freddy and Harmy decided the best way to cope was by drinking with the Aussies until midnight, which upset Duncan even more. He didn't want us to socialise with them until the end of the series, if at all, and in his mind it wasn't a coincidence that our two best players, Collingwood and Pietersen, were the two most likely to get in Australia's faces.

The media reaction was worse than it would have been if we'd been hammered again. Losing like that exasperates pundits. If you get thrashed there's an air of weariness and resignation about the press's response. A defeat like this causes people to lash out in frustration and anger.

No amount of media training can help in this situation, because there is no right answer. Whatever you say leaves you open to attack: Freddie was laughed at for saying we'd played well for four days, even though it was true; Duncan was 'blasted' for not showing enough emotion.

And suddenly it all seemed irrelevant when Ashley got the news his wife Stine was suffering from a brain tumour. He flew home immediately.

Stine underwent a six-hour operation that saved her life. She made a full recovery and founded The Giles Trust, which raises funds for research into brain tumours.

***

This was the last way I wanted to get my place back, but even before he'd heard the news, Ashley was struggling. It's easy to shut out the media when the critic is manifestly an idiot, like the one who thought I was dishonouring Indira Gandhi for eating an Indian takeaway while wearing a patka. It's not as easy when you're getting pummelled by every pundit on the circuit, including quite a few who were singing your praises only a fortnight earlier. Even Graham Thorpe was getting stuck into Ashley, and the two of them had been close on previous tours when Ashley had spent hours helping Graham when he'd been struggling with personal issues.

It was getting to Geraint Jones, too. He was never quite as popular with the public as he was with his teammates, but he was a Duncan kind of player, someone who had an edge to him. Geraint was happy to get verbally stuck into the Aussies, but he was struggling with the bat and that affects anyone's confidence.

Duncan's Chrisreadophobia meant the selectors felt they had to give Geraint another game, but I was pretty sure I was going to be selected for the third Test in Perth even before we knew Ashley was going home.

Back in England, people were jamming Radio Five's switchboard, demanding that I should be included. That was more likely to make Duncan ignore me than select me, but by then he'd come to the conclusion he had to drop Ashley.

As gutted as I was to see us lose in Adelaide, because I wasn't directly responsible (except by omission) it didn't have the psychological effect on me that it had on some of the others.

It was still a thrill to hear Freddie say 'Eleven, Panesar' when he was reading the team sheet out and that was maybe the point.

At that stage in my career I was still thrilled by the idea of playing an Ashes Test match. It didn't matter to me that we were 2-0 down with three to play and that our chances of retaining the Ashes were being written off. My head was right. I hadn't yet experienced the kind of doubt that was affecting Geraint and, unbeknownst to us at the time, Freddie.

On my Ashes debut I took 5-92, getting rid of Justin Langer, Andrew Symonds, Adam Gilchrist, Shane Warne and Brett Lee – three world-class batsmen and two high-class lower order players.

Langer was my first Ashes wicket and I celebrated it nearly as wildly as I had when I had removed Sachin twenty months earlier.

For an innings I felt like I was in a state of grace. When Shane Warne came out he congratulated me for the delivery that had brought him to the crease when Ian Bell caught Gilchrist at short leg.

'Well bowled, mate. That was a good ball.'

If he'd known how great it made me feel to hear him say that he might have thought twice about it, although then again, probably not. Warnie was always fair.

We got them all out for 244 and morale was soaring. Then they got us for 215 and morale was no longer soaring. I took three wickets in the second innings but went for 145 runs. I at least got Mike Hussey, but as he'd already made 103, I'm not sure I can claim I won that round of the Wantage Road Clasico.

The good news was that we made one of the ten highest second innings totals ever recorded by an England team. The bad news was that we still lost by 206 runs, and I had the questionable honour of being the batsman out when they clinched the series as Warnie bowled me.

This time we were more resigned than disappointed and we were hammered in Melbourne, where I bowled twelve wicketless overs. Sydney wasn't quite as bad and I took 2-90, but we still lost by ten wickets.

It was a 5-0 whitewash and Mike Selvey of *The Guardian* called it 'England's greatest humiliation in eighty-six years'. Australia hadn't beaten us 5-0 since 1921, when the team travelled by boat and the English press tried to make excuses for the margin of defeat by claiming Australia's players had recovered more quickly from the First World War than ours had.

The 2006–2007 press corps wasn't as forgiving. Freddie defended us, saying he couldn't have asked for any more from us and that we'd been 'beaten by the better team'. That was true, but they didn't want to know.

Duncan pointed out that some of the flak we were getting came from pundits who had played during the eighties, when England had won three Ashes series against far weaker Australian sides (sides he himself had played against for Zimbabwe). His benchmark for that era was the West Indies, against whom England didn't win a single Test for over a decade. He had a point.

The trouble was that after a 5-0 series defeat, no one really wanted reasoned analysis. They wanted a blood sacrifice.

After the Melbourne defeat the ECB decided the solution was to ask a golfer called Ken Schofield to hold a few meetings and find out what had gone wrong.

The Schofield Report sounded like the title for a dull-sounding current affairs programme and Duncan knew nothing about it until Mike Atherton dropped a reference to it into an interview after the Sydney Test.

It was an inquest waiting for a victim.

My mum, Gursharan, and my dad, Paramjit (whom we call Bob the Builder) at a family function in 1998.

At home, aged ten, in full kit, but looking distinctly underwhelmed. I wasn't always obsessed with cricket and once cried on my way to a match.

On the Under-19 tour to India, with Chris Tremlett, Rob Ferley, Ian Pattison, Gary Pratt and Nicky Peng.

Playing for Northants in Division 2 of the County Championship, back in 2003. My county career took a while to get going, because I often had exams that coincided with the start of the season.

The sheer joy of claiming my first wicket at Nagpur against India in 2006. It isn't true that I had a premonition I'd get Sachin Tendulkar out and the celebrations were completely spontaneous. I just couldn't believe it!

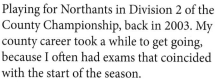

The first Test against Sri Lanka at Lord's in 2006. I was getting as swept up in Monty Mania as everyone else!

Leaving the field with Harmy and Hoggy after bowling Pakistan out for 504 during the third Test at The Oval, August 2006. At that point we had absolutely no idea that a ball-tampering scandal was about to engulf the series.

Umpires Darrell Hair (centre) and Billy Doctrove (left) examining the match ball with Pakistan captain Inzamam-ul-Haq during the fourth day of the fourth Test match. I always got on well with Darrell Hair, but this saga ended his career and he would later be affected by mental health issues.

Meeting the Queen during the tea break at Lord's, May 2007. Her Majesty was a lovely, gentle human being.

Celebrating my Man of the Match award with Michael Vaughan after beating the West Indies in the third Test at Old Trafford, June 2007. Even now, twelve years on, I still think of Vaughany as my captain; he was a natural leader.

Celebrating the wicket of New Zealand captain Daniel Vettori at Old Trafford in 2008, when I took my best single innings figures of 6/37.

With England captain Andrew Flintoff during England's 2008 tour to India. Freddie and I clicked straight away. He was, and is, an inspiration and a brilliant human being.

Good old Sussex by the sea? Moving counties worked well for a while, but behind the scenes trouble was brewing. I was becoming paranoid and convinced my teammates were dropping catches on purpose.

The miracle of Cardiff. Jimmy and I celebrate after our Dunkirk-like escape in the first Ashes Test. I was euphoric, but I also knew I was almost certainly going to be dropped. I never played another home Test match.

Enjoying a joke with Graeme Swann during a net session in Johannesburg, January 2010. Swanny's a naturally funny guy, with a relentless, piss-taking English sense of humour. You had to know how to take it. Kepler Wessels didn't!

Bombed out by Sussex after my infamous night out in Brighton, I moved to Essex. It should have revived my career, but instead my paranoia got worse, culminating in a furious row with James Foster.

I was due to partner Melody LeMoal on *Dancing on Ice*, only to wreck my ankle trying a jump during rehearsals.

I didn't get to dance on ice, but I did play cricket on it: here I am with Graeme Smith at the 2018 Cricket on Ice event in Switzerland.

With Piers Morgan and Susanna Reid in the GMTV studio. Piers is a huge cricket fan and I'm a regular on the GMTV sofa.

In the *MasterChef* studio, getting ready to cremate a salmon.

My fellow *Celebrity MasterChef* contestants, the actor Chizzy Akudolu and the Paralympian Stef Reid.

With my great friend Harbhajan Singh in the Media Centre at Lord's, during the second Test against India, 2018.

Style icon? In my Paul Jheeta jacket.

Rambo.

Chapter 16

A Pawn in Someone Else's Chess Match

To everyone's surprise, including ours, we won the ODI series that followed the Ashes. I hadn't expected to play any part. I'd barely played any one-day cricket for Northants and when David Graveney rang me towards the end of the Ashes series to say I was in the squad, I had to stop myself from asking him why he'd picked me.

Even now I'm still not quite sure how we managed to win a tri-nations series despite losing four of our first five games. It's not as if we lost them by narrow margins. They weren't even close. By the time Australia had beaten us by nine wickets on Australia Day, the remaining hacks covering the tour had run out of superlatives to describe how bad we were. Duncan was reduced to apologising to supporters and Ian Bell said we'd hit rock bottom.

He was premature. We still managed to lose to New Zealand by 58 runs in the next game but Paul Nixon and Liam Plunkett had a dart towards the end and denied the Kiwis a bonus point, meaning we could still theoretically sneak into the final.

We were so bad it lulled Australia into a false sense of security. For the next match, John Buchanan rested Ponting, Lee and McGrath, which probably wouldn't have offended anyone, given that they'd already qualified for the finals, if Buchanan hadn't said that neither we nor New Zealand were testing his team.

If you looked at the performances it was probably true, but it absolutely incensed Duncan. He thought Buchanan was humiliating us and it motivated him and us to one final act of defiance. We won the next four matches and with it, the trophy.

I played in both finals and found myself in the squad for the World Cup.

Like a number of aspects of my career, this didn't pan out exactly as I'd imagined it would.

The opening ceremony was great, but it kind of tailed off from there. Morale was good after the way we'd finished the Australia Tour and even after we'd lost to New Zealand in the group match in St Lucia, we were still in with a good chance of qualifying for the knock-out phase.

I went to bed that night oblivious to what was going on a short distance from the hotel. That was because I was also oblivious to what was going on in the hotel, where Freddie had been climbing the walls after the defeat.

His way of coping was to go out. He found some of the younger members of the squad and was drinking till around 1.30 am. At this point, with the others flagging, he decided he wanted to carry on drinking. With Ian Botham.

The problem was that Botham, he thought, was on a boat that was a bit too far for him to swim to, given his condition. He decided it was safer to take a pedalo instead, but he slipped over and ended up in a few inches of water. He then got up and went back to the hotel.

It was a fairly mundane incident but it was reported like the biggest maritime disaster since the sinking of the *Mary Rose*. The real problem was that it wasn't his first offence. During the Australia tour he'd been out until 7 am, again with Beefy, and Duncan had nearly stripped him of his job when he was still drunk at training.

I didn't realise at the time that I'd been a bone of contention for them. Freddie claimed Duncan told him to make me field at backward point during a one-dayer because he wanted to expose me. Freddie wanted to put me somewhere like third man, where my failings wouldn't be as obvious. It seemed I'd become a pawn in Duncan's chess match with the other selectors.

Two days after the incident, Freddie gave a press conference where he apologised profusely. There are times when you hear a public apology from a sports star or a politician and you know it's a calculated act to try to mitigate the punishment. Not with Freddie. He threw himself into the apology with the same gusto he'd thrown himself into almost everything else he did. He knew he shouldn't have been out that late and he felt he'd let everyone down. When he said he was ashamed and embarrassed, we all knew he meant it. It was a feeling I'd have to come to terms with later in my career. Unfortunately, shame and embarrassment aren't an ideal mindset for a professional sportsman.

The knock-on effect was that Duncan was once again steaming with anger when he should have been focusing on getting us ready for the next match, and Michael Vaughan was getting increasingly tense.

The levity had gone from the squad. Even those of us who hadn't been out felt we couldn't really be seen laughing any more. Some newspapers regard enjoying yourself as a crime in a time of national crisis.

It was a night out that went wrong. Most people know what that feels like (and my time would come on that front). The furore over this drunken incident was put into perspective by what happened over the next forty-eight hours.

The day after we lost to New Zealand, Pakistan were beaten by Ireland in one of the biggest upsets in the tournament's history. The following morning, their coach, Bob Woolmer, was found dead in his hotel room and within a couple of days a false theory that he'd been murdered started to spread.

Most of our squad knew Bob. I don't think there was anyone on the circuit who had a bad word to say about him and the idea that he might have been killed because Pakistan had lost sent a chill through the tournament.

That story turned out to be false but it was obvious Vaughan wasn't enjoying the tournament any more. His captaincy style was based on the idea that cricket was supposed to be fun, but there was a serious goal at the end of it. The ethos was that it didn't matter if you lost, as long as you did everything you could to win.

Now it was all work and no play. Because we couldn't be seen to be having fun any more, the pressure built and the team got nervous. We lost when it mattered and won when it didn't.

Elimination meant the end for Duncan. I think by then he'd had enough anyway, but he told us he was leaving before the dead rubber with the West Indies in Barbados. He didn't say a lot but he didn't have to. The tears in his eyes were a reminder that he was as human as everyone else.

Vaughan was welling up too. I don't think you can overstate what English cricket owes these two men. For the 2005 Ashes series alone they could have been knighted, but their achievements went well beyond that. Duncan took a team that was trapped in a cycle of mediocrity and failure and gave an entire generation of cricket fans memories that will last for a lifetime.

For me personally, I've no doubt that he made me a better cricketer and a better person.

I always liked Duncan. I'm just not sure he liked me! Actually, I'm pretty sure he did. He'd always say, 'Monty, it's easier to destroy a player than it is to make him better.' He absolutely made me a better player. Wherever he is in the world now, I wish him well.

Chapter 17

'What are Your Processes?'

A man's got to know his limitations.

Clint Eastwood to Hal Holbrooke,
Magnum Force

Duncan's replacement, Peter Moores, had a boundless enthusiasm for cricket, and that was one of the reasons for his downfall. Cricketers of a certain age don't like enthusiasm. It's too exhausting.

It was normal for Duncan to go hours or even days without speaking to you, but Peter was in your face almost the whole time. KP said he was like a woodpecker, hammering away at his head, and Michael Vaughan ended up retiring when we might have enjoyed him for another couple of years.

Mooresy was one of the game's great enthusiasts, and that works well for a young cricketer at the start of his career but less well for a senior pro like, say, Phil Tufnell, who prays his side will win the toss and bat so he can put his feet up with a cup of tea and a fag.

By that stage of my career I was probably somewhere in the middle: a 25-year-old who was looking to build on my early successes and push on in my mission to become The Greatest Spin Bowler in the World.

Peter was a genuinely nice guy and an honourable man who refused to get dragged into slanging matches when some of his former players were having a go at him. I liked him a lot, but when he took over the culture shock was so acute it was tantamount to a full-scale 'regime change'.

There's an episode in the fourth series of *Blackadder* that reminds me of one of the first conversations I had with Peter after he was appointed. General Melchett, the character played by Stephen Fry, comes down to the trenches and asks Baldrick a question: 'Ah, tally-ho, yippety-dip and zing zang spillip! Looking forward to bullying off for the final chukka?'

He doesn't reply, so Rowan Atkinson says, 'Answer the General, Baldrick.'

To which Baldrick responds, 'I can't answer him, Sir, I don't know what he's talking about.'

I'd had a brief spell with Peter at the Academy before going to India in 2006, but I didn't know him that well, so when he asked me, 'Monty, what are your processes?' I had my Baldrick moment.

I didn't have a fucking clue how to answer him! So I pretended I'd misheard to buy a few more seconds of thinking time.

'Sorry, Peter?'

'What are your processes?'

This one, innocent question capsized my brain.

What are my *processes*?

What are *my* processes?

What *are* my processes?

Not for the first time in my life, someone with my entire future in his hands had asked me something he obviously thought was important and I'd no idea how to answer him. Even now, over a decade later, I still don't know how to answer that question. I'm not even sure there is a right answer.

Maybe I should have said, 'I pitch the ball in a good area, six times out of six and get it to turn,' but I just stammered a reply. I was so incoherent he might well have thought I was on something and I'm pretty sure he walked away thinking that I didn't know my game.

In hindsight, I think he wanted to know what my technique was, but technique was never my problem. At least not when it came to my bowling …

***

The public image of Peter was that he was a robot who was obsessed by statistics. The reality wasn't as simplistic as that, but he wanted England to follow the same kind of map he'd used at Sussex, when Chris Adams was his captain.

Adams was an outspoken character, who was very competitive and, like Vaughan, always backed his teammates up if they had any run-ins with the opposition. In domestic cricket, their 'processes' worked … brilliantly. Sussex had been a backwater until Peter became coach, but he took them into Division One in 2001 and won them their first ever title in 2003, after 164 years. Where Peter got it wrong was in thinking that what worked in county cricket would also work at international level.

He was dealing with better players, bigger egos and crucially, the ageing process.

I remember speaking to some of the younger players on the tour to New Zealand and they were saying that he was great because his methods involved getting the absolute maximum out of players in all three disciplines: batting, bowling and fielding.

That works at county level because almost every player has the potential to improve, but the England squad of that era included players who had already peaked and were struggling with injuries that in some cases would eventually end their careers. For players in their thirties, the need for constant, ongoing development proved self-defeating and it probably forced Michael Vaughan into premature retirement.

Vaughan was the best captain I ever had. He exuded natural authority, had obvious leadership qualities and was a wonderful, elegant batsman.

When Peter took over, Vaughan was thirty-two. This is an age when some batsmen are entering their prime, but Vaughan had been suffering from knee pain ever since he was a teenager. His cartilage had been trimmed when he was eighteen and by now he was on his fourth operation. Cartilage doesn't repair itself so his knee needed to be managed, but Peter remembered that Vaughany had been a decent off-spinner earlier in his career and he wanted him to start turning his arm over again.

It was a reasonable idea in theory as Vaughan had taken over 100 first class wickets, but his knee wouldn't withstand the impact of landing as he came in to bowl. Vaughan knew this and tried to explain it to Peter, but I don't think he can have realised how serious his condition was as he kept pushing him to bowl.

Peter was forty-four years of age but he was still phenomenally fit, so maybe he didn't understand how the ageing process affected mere mortals. He should have kept pushing the youngsters, while leaving the older players to play however they wanted to, because after so many years there's only so much you can do physically. You don't have the same energy levels when you're thirty-five that you have when you're twenty-five.

When Arsene Wenger took over at Highbury, he knew his defenders were all over thirty so he looked after them because he knew they could perform when it mattered. By giving Tony Adams a different training regime to Thierry Henry, he managed to get another five full seasons out of him, even though he was suffering with injuries. If Peter had used the same approach with Michael Vaughan, he might have got another two or three years out of him and the fiasco of his fall-out with KP might never have happened.

Personally, I was, at least, able to enjoy one English summer playing under Vaughan, during which I showed that there wasn't a lot wrong with my processes. I was man-of-the-series as we beat the West Indies 3-0, taking twenty-three wickets and getting my name on the honours board.

We also got to meet the Queen and Prince Philip before the Lord's Test. Her Majesty seemed like a very gentle, lovely human being and the Duke knows his cricket. He'd captained an England Invitational XI when he was a younger man. We also knew he had a reputation for making 'gaffes', like the time he went to Scotland and asked a driving instructor if he could keep the natives off the booze long enough for them to pass their driving test! Or the time he said he might catch a 'ghastly disease' if he stroked a koala while on a state visit to Australia.

As the first Sikh to play for England I did wonder if he might make the kind of joke that would get him into the papers again, but he was just very friendly, saying that he remembered when I'd made my debut. In any case, people seem to forgive Prince Philip his gaffes. Mainly because, I think, he's joking, and there's no malice intended.

Compare and contrast the Prince Philip approach with the Norman Tebbit approach: I don't think anyone thought the cricket test interview was a joke, mainly because whenever Tebbit spoke he did so in a style that made Duncan Fletcher look like Michael McIntyre.

***

For me personally, the India series that followed was more emotionally charged. It always was when I played against them, although I think my India-based relatives were more conflicted than I was. I wanted to win every game I played in, regardless of who it was against, but I'd had family members like my granddad who were now willing me to take wickets against the team they'd always supported.

Actually taking those wickets was easier said than done. It was a damp summer and the pitches we'd prepared weren't offering any help against opponents like Dravid, Tendulkar and Laxman, who were among the best players of spin in the world.

Weirdly enough, my opposite number, Anil Kumble, topped their averages, with an amazing fifty-four.

We should have got at least a draw out of the series, but a mixture of bad luck and the weather thwarted us, while I took a relatively modest 8-403 over the three matches. We probably would have won the first Test at Lord's but we knew the rain was coming on day five and couldn't get the final wicket. When I look back at the footage of my appeal, when I hit Sreesanth on the pad as the light was fading, I almost frightened myself. It was like my eyes were about to pop out of their sockets.

I'd been told unofficially that I needed to tone it down a bit during the West Indies series but in that situation, desperation kicks in.

I was absolutely convinced I had him, and there would be occasions later in my career when I did let my disappointment get the better of me. Again, it's a human reaction, although that's an explanation, not an excuse.

I took 4-101 at Trent Bridge, but we lost by seven wickets and we all struggled in the final Test at The Oval, where Kumble made 110 not out. We held on for the draw but lost the series 1-0.

It wasn't a disgraceful performance but any series defeat leaves people asking questions and pointing fingers. And in the background there was serious trouble brewing between some of the senior players and Peter Moores.

Chapter 18

No Salad Dodgers

Towards the end of our Indian summer a media squall broke out when Duncan – a man of so few words at times he seemed to be preparing for an after-cricket career in a Trappist monastery – suddenly produced over 100,000 of them in an autobiography.

Seven years' worth of pent-up frustration spilled out onto the pages. It was like he'd filed every grievance he'd ever had in a hard drive stored in his brain and his autobiography was the result.

Behind the Shades read like a score-settling exercise. He'd been subjected to a lot of criticism during his tenure as England coach and this was his chance to answer back, liberated from the restrictions placed on him by his contract with the ECB.

As we were still obliged to adhere to the terms of our contracts, it wasn't easy to respond. Officially the line was that Duncan was entitled to his opinions and that his criticisms wouldn't affect us.

Unofficially? Even if the number of cricketers who read it cover to cover is small, a book like that is about as welcome in the dressing room as a Jim Davidson tribute act in a Sikh temple. In fact, I can imagine this book going down similarly well in Norman Tebbit's office in the House of Lords.

Some cricketers are big readers, others aren't. I read a lot of coaching manuals and cricket history when I was younger, but I didn't read autobiographies. You didn't have to because as soon as one was published, the entire press pack would be devouring it in a single sitting and looking for anything that might make a headline.

Then you'd get asked a question along the lines of 'Did it hurt when your former batting partner said you were the least professional cricketer he'd ever clapped eyes on?'

And all you can say is, 'He's entitled to his opinion and it won't affect my game.'

You can, however, get 'a close friend' to talk on your behalf. Or your dad. Freddie couldn't say what he really felt about Fletcher exposing his drinking on tour, but he could get his dad to tell *The Telegraph* he'd been 'betrayed'.

The funny thing is, I don't think Duncan actually disliked any of his players, even if it might have come across that way. We frustrated him at times but there was nothing in the book that he wouldn't say to our faces.

The media, however, were a different matter. Geoff Boycott and Ian Botham got it with both barrels and Duncan revealed at one point that he'd confronted Henry Blofeld, only for Blowers to tell him to 'fuck off'. He didn't even say 'Fuck off, my dear old thing.'

Duncan disliked retired professionals who he felt were inconsistent and at times hypocritical. As these made up a significant percentage of the press pack that followed England around, they copped a lot of the criticism. This in turn wound up the journalists, who filleted his book for headlines and found plenty when it came to his attitude towards his players. Especially me.

Nick Cook took a blast for Northants' failure to turn me into Jonty Rhodes and for 'sending me to England without an arm ball'. There was nothing new in finding out he didn't rate me as a batsman or a fielder, but even the compliment about me being the 'best finger spinner in the world' seemed to have been bowled from the back of his hand.

He'd meant it when he said it; he just didn't think there was any real competition around, other than Daniel Vettori and Nicky Boje.

You could have compiled a pretty good XI from the players he'd had a go at. Freddie would have been the captain, Chris Read would have kept wicket and I'd have been the spinner.

I was obviously asked to comment, which was awkward. This was something else they'd forgotten to put on the values card: what to do when a former coach says you're no better than Nicky Boje.

An interviewer from *The Guardian* asked me how long it had taken to finish his book. I said I hadn't even bothered to pick it up, which was true, and that I had no interest in it, which was slightly less true.

I had no interest in actually sitting down and reading it, but I was interested in what he'd had to say. You always are when it comes from someone you respect. It's easy to brush off criticism when it comes from a heckler in Bay 13 who's on his sixteenth can of Fosters, but when it's from a man who gave you your England debut, it stings a bit.

If it hadn't stung I probably wouldn't have given an interview to the *Mail*, in which I implied his coaching of spin bowlers wasn't as great as it could have been, but in hindsight I didn't think any of the things he'd said about me were unfair. I did wonder what he'd done with the 'values' card they'd given us though. Maybe he'd burned his copy.

***

Another theme of Duncan's book was his contempt for players who were physically unprepared for modern cricket. One of the many things he did for English cricket was to leave us with our fittest ever generation of players. The days when you could prepare for a series with the Larkins Diet, a strict regime of alcohol and nicotine, were long gone, but even as late as the mid-nineties, Mike Atherton was still having to hide as many as six fielders, because they were either unfit, butter-fingered, or both.

There were no salad dodgers in Duncan's teams and players who were naturally inclined to put on weight had to work ferociously hard to stay in shape.

Peter, however, wanted us to go even harder, and it pushed some of the squad to breaking point and beyond.

The Sri Lanka tour in December 2007 was physically and mentally draining. My figures, 8-405, were almost identical to those from the India series and the end result was the same as we lost the series 1-0, but any similarities ended there.

The Sri Lankans didn't hammer me, but they broke me slowly – Mahela Jayawardene in particular.

We actually started OK in the first Test, getting them all out for 188 in the first innings. In the space of five overs I removed Jayawardene, Vaas and Fernando, and we ended up with a 93-run lead, but the second time around they were ready for us.

Sangakkara in particular was imperious, making 152 and realistically putting the game beyond us. I bowled for forty-five overs on a dead track, taking three wickets but going for 132.

They set us a target of 350, which we were never going to get anyway near. The only encouragement was that the track was so lifeless even Murali was struggling on it, although the word 'struggling' is relative when it comes to Murali.

Matt Prior and Ian Bell batted so well that at one point we thought we might see out a draw, but with around half an hour before the light was due to fade, Murali got them both in the space of a couple of overs. We ended up losing by 88 runs.

We hadn't disgraced ourselves but in some ways the second Test in Colombo was worse, even though we drew. We batted first, made 351 and then went through a kind of cricketing purgatory as they made 548-9. I got Jayawardene, caught by Paul Collingwood, but only after he'd made 195.

It was Guantanamo cricket, played out on the sort of wicket where hope goes to die.

By the time they'd declared, even Dilhara Fernando had been able to make 36 not out and there was nothing left for us to do but bat out the draw.

We drew again in Galle and by now we were going backwards. This time, Jayawardene made 213 and he seemed to know exactly what I was going to do before I even knew it myself. I bowled twenty-five overs without taking a wicket, then got myself run out when Steve Harmison clipped one off his legs. He set off and I stood my ground until I realised, 'He isn't going back.'

For a second I thought we might be OK as the throw was poor, but Jayawardene gathered it and managed to hit the stumps with only one to aim at. We were all out for 81 and the incident didn't do anything to enhance my reputation as a tail-ender.

We were six down when the rain saved us in the second innings, and other than Alastair Cook, who'd made 118, no one really had any reason to celebrate.

When we'd lost 1-0 to India in the summer, we knew we'd been unlucky. Here we knew we could easily have been whitewashed and morale was collapsing. Some of the senior players were on the brink.

Vaughan was still struggling with his knee and his form was dipping. Duncan's philosophy was that if you were being asked to captain and play as a specialist batsman, you were effectively an all-rounder, but in practice, even a player like Vaughan loses confidence if he's struggling for runs.

Matthew Hoggard was under pressure after a couple of bad Tests and unbeknownst to any of us, he was starting to suffer from depression. KP was getting stressed out because of the relentlessness of the schedule. Even after playing a game, we'd still have to do a fitness session and somehow find time for a team meeting.

In a portent of what was to come he went to Peter Moores and said we needed to have fewer meetings, because they were doing his head in. KP loved cricket as much as anyone in the squad, but he couldn't consume it intravenously, 24-7.

Moores listened to what he had to say, took it on board and apparently ignored it completely.

We went home for Christmas and tried to recuperate for the trip to New Zealand, a tour that would finish another great cricketer's career.

Chapter 19

'If You Want My Advice ...'

The best advice I ever received was from a man wearing a Panama hat, a tank top and an immaculate suit in a lift at Headingley.

As this was Yorkshire, he didn't feel the need to say either 'hello' or 'good morning', and as he was a man who needed no introduction, he didn't bother introducing himself. He just came straight out with it.

'Ah've got woon piece of adviiiise for you.'

I could already tell he was going to tell me what it was whether I liked it or not.

'You're a natural bowler, you're fantastic, you've got aaaall the attributes to be a great spinner ...'

I suspected there was a 'but' coming. Instead he kept it brief and characteristically blunt.

'The second word is off. You work out the rest.'

'Ok Geoff,' I nodded. 'I will.'

And I should have, at least, in so many words.

The problem was that I also loved cricket, so if I had the chance to pick the brains of someone I respected, I'd pick them. If I had the chance to ask Nasser Hussain, Shaun Udal, John Emburey or Bishan Bedi for advice, I'd ask them.

The problem with asking so many different people for advice is that unless there's a consensus, it becomes contradictory, and can end up doing more harm than good. Is Legend A's opinion worth more than Legend B's?

I had more mentors then I could count. What I needed was one single voice that I could trust. Duncan had once said to me that if I ever got stuck in international cricket and needed a loyal man as a friend and a guide, I should go to Nasser Hussain.

I did, but I kept asking other people for advice as well, and it all contributed to my tendency to overthink things.

It was around about this time that Shane Warne made his quip about me playing the same Test match thirty-three times. That remark got into my head and it was still there a year later when I was bowling to Australia at Cardiff and getting nowhere. That was the genius of Warne: there aren't many players who can still help their batsmen two years after they've retired!

***

My problem varied on who you listened to. People like Mike Selvey thought I was treading water. In a piece for *The Guardian* he wrote: 'Monty appeared to learn not one single thing from the [Sri Lanka] trip, which rather sums up his international career: he began it as a very good bowler and he remains just that, stuck on the same level at which he started.'

Selvey cited a specific problem - that Jayawardene knew exactly what I was going to do: 'Monty bowls off-stumpish and good length. Jayawardene plonks his left leg forward and waits until the ball is under his nose, at which point his left hand rotates the bat blade clockwise an eighth of a turn, his right deftly imparts a little energy and the ball slides away through point in the direction of a distant fielder. The batsmen stroll a single and the scoreboard clicks round. It happened time after time after time ...'

Being too predictable can seriously harm a bowler.

This was Saqlain Mushtaq's problem later in his career. When he first delivered the doosra it brought him a glut of wickets and everyone tried to copy him. I spent hours in the nets trying to replicate what he did, but I never managed to get it right, or at least not often enough for it to be worth bowling.

I knew if I tried it in a match situation I'd end up going for too many runs, so I reluctantly gave up on the idea. In the meantime, the word was getting around the circuit and Saqlain's doosra was getting easier to spot. From then on, his career went into relative decline.

On the other hand, predictability never did Glenn McGrath any harm. He could have bowled faster than he did, but he had phenomenal discipline. McGrath knew the ball would bounce more if he dropped his pace to 4–5 mph below his maximum. The batsman always knew exactly where the ball was going to land, but he didn't know if it would rear up or skid through to the wicketkeeper. In the end he just ground people out. Shane Warne called it the torture method.

Murali was another player who could do a lot more with the ball than he actually did during matches, because he concentrated on what would get wickets. His fingers were so powerful that he could actually bowl a ball so that it turned at a right angle. The drawback with that was that even if you managed to land it right at the bowling crease, you'd only have one stump to aim at. It was the equivalent of the kind of trick shot that a snooker player can do in an exhibition match but would never dream of playing in a tournament.

Ashley Giles summed the problem up for me: it wasn't that I didn't have the variations, I was just trying too many. A bowler needs to create doubt in the batsman's mind, not his own. In the end, cricket is a bit like paper-scissors-stone: as long as the batsman doesn't know which of three balls might be coming, you've got a chance of getting him out.

As far as Geoffrey Boycott's advice went, at that time in my life I wasn't the kind of person who could walk around telling people to fuck off. Although it was something I'd get better at with time.

Chapter 20

Like Getting Punched

Friedrich Nietzsche said 'What doesn't kill you makes you stronger,' but he'd never been touring with Peter Moores.

Flying to New Zealand does strange things to both the mind and the body. Even with the shortest possible connection time it still takes over a day to get there, flying across multiple time zones. You arrive disorientated by the jet lag and weary from being in the air all that time, even if you haven't been sitting next to Wayne Larkins.

I arrived in Auckland for our 2008 tour a couple of weeks after the players who'd been selected for the limited overs games and it was obvious some of them were struggling with the schedule. You could see it in their eyes. Weariness, exhaustion and fatigue.

More worryingly, in Vaughan's case the spark was going out. The man who'd put the fun back into English cricket was having it slowly extracted.

KP was never great at hiding his irritation, but he was at least letting out his frustration.

Sometimes it's the quiet ones you have to watch and that's especially true when you're on tour.

After our first fitness session I realised why everyone had the thousand-yard stare. I was absolutely gone. I was twenty-five years old and in theory I was physically in the prime of my life, but during Peter's training sessions it felt like we were being fucking punched for not being fit enough. I was in bits. It was like we were in the final selection for the SAS, running until we were on the brink of collapse.

I coped, but I had a good base level of fitness and I was injury-free. I'd also missed the one day series, during which the team were doing training sessions after matches while New Zealand were enjoying a few beers. KP said they were just laughing at us from the balcony.

We'd fly between venues, get off the plane and somehow immediately end up doing a training session. Wherever we landed, it always seemed to be near to a mountain Peter wanted us to run up. It was Full Metal Jacket drill instructor stuff – push-ups, squat thrusts, shuttle runs, sprints and even exercises where we were made to carry each other.

You could see KP steaming with anger: 'What's the fucking point, China?' Then the fat-shaming started.

'Ok lads, I want you to strip down to your underpants. We're going to take some pictures of you.'

You can imagine how well that went down. We were cricketers, not Chippendales. Apparently they wanted to assess how our body shapes changed during the course of the tour. This was culturally awkward. Ever seen a Sikh version of *The Full Monty*?

Physically I was young enough to cope with the training and mentally I was still OK, but what was happening behind the scenes with Matthew Hoggard proved that Marcus's case wasn't a one-off.

Hoggy had always been there for me on the field. If I was bowling and I needed reassurance that it was coming out OK, I'd look to him. I'd see him at mid-on or mid-off and he'd be saying, 'Bounce! Bounce! Bounce!'

He had a dry, Yorkshire sense of humour and I never had an inkling that he was suffering. In his case, his wife Sarah had been struggling with depression even before she gave birth to their son Ernie. She was then hit by post-natal depression as well, and the situation was only exacerbated by the fact that her husband was on the other side of the world.

In the first Test at Hamilton, Hoggy was about to run in to bowl when he started welling up. He alerted Vaughan and said, 'I think I'm going cuckoo, I think I'm doing a Tres.' He held it together for long enough to complete the game, but that was the end of his international career. The selectors made the decision and Vaughan and Moores had to deliver the news. We were in the nets at Wellington when he was told. He just said, 'Right, cheers,' and that was it.

When you're a young cricketer obsessed with your own game you don't always empathise with a player who's been dropped, but I'd find out what he was going through soon enough. If you look at it coldly, you can argue it made sense. Jimmy Anderson and Stuart Broad were coming through and even as I write this a decade later, they remain the outstanding bowling partnership in Test cricket. It was the brutality of it that seems striking in hindsight. He'd taken 248 Test wickets and although he said he used to just 'shut his eyes and wang it', he must have had more to offer.

It says something for Vaughan's man-management skills that I didn't even know about the Hamilton incident until Hoggy wrote about it a year later. I don't think any of the team did. Marcus's condition had been impossible to hide, but with Hoggy, because this one incident had happened out in the middle, it seemed to be swept under the carpet. I think he felt the selectors held it against him, however, and you have to wonder about the affect it had on Vaughan. You have to make some cold decisions as a captain and I doubt he made any colder than this one, jettisoning a teammate who'd been with him for years and who'd helped him achieve some of the greatest moments in his career.

Hoggy had entered that limbo all dropped cricketers enter, when you know that being dropped isn't necessarily the end but that with every match that passes, your chances of a recall diminish.

Chapter 21

The Harmison Paradox

After Freddie and Marcus, Hoggy was the third last person I would have believed would suffer from mental health issues.

With Steve Harmison it wasn't such a surprise. His case is unusual because with many cricketers, mental health issues stem from a feeling that the game is slipping away from you, especially as you get older and your performance levels dip, or your injuries force you to give up completely.

For a while, Harmy actually was The Greatest Fast Bowler in the World, but he couldn't cope with the side effects of his own brilliance - specifically, the need to spend half the year away from his family. He was a lovely guy, but he never seemed happy on tour, for the simple reason that he usually wasn't. Harmy might well have had a much happier life if he hadn't been such a wonderful bowler.

He was lucky enough to meet the love of his life when he was a teenager and he became a father at nineteen. If he'd been an average cricketer, he might have played for a league side at the weekends, done a nine-to-five job in Ashington and raised his four kids in a state of domestic bliss.

The standard joke about Harmy was that he thought the equator went through Gateshead and that he needed jabs if he went as far as South Shields. He was an easy target though, and in hindsight perhaps it was too easy. If he was happy in Ashington, what was wrong with that?

A cricketer's first tour can be a rite of passage for a young, single man but when Harmy went to Pakistan with the Under-19s, he already had someone to miss back in England and he ended up flying home early. The experience of being separated from his wife left scars that never fully healed and unbeknownst to all of us, he'd suffered a breakdown similar to Marcus's before the 2004 tour to South Africa.

It wasn't something I fully understood at the time. I didn't have children and it was only when I became an uncle early in 2018 that I began to understand in a small way what the cricketers who had children were going through.

We attributed Harmy's obvious unhappiness to homesickness. On his happier tours his room was like an expat pub, with the alcohol keeping cool in the bath. He'd rig up a dartboard and get all the English football matches on his laptop, so it was almost like a social hub for the rest of the boys. Swanny called it 'The Harmison Arms' and he was a great landlord, the life and soul right up until closing time, when everyone went home and he'd start climbing the walls again.

His behaviour was more demonstrative than Hoggard's. For a start he didn't have a poker face. When he smiled it was contagious and when he was down it was pretty clear from his body language, although at that point there was no indication that he'd been contemplating self-harm.

He was also really sensitive to criticism. This was something else that should have been part of our media training. There should, for example, have been a module on how to deal with Geoff Boycott.

Boycott was all right; you just had to know how to take him. He was the sort of pundit who'd shower you with praise when you did well and lash you with his mother's stick of rhubarb if you weren't performing. It wasn't personal with Boycott, but Harmy took it that way and he once told him to his face to fuck off. Following the advice Geoffrey once gave me to the letter, in fact.

The vocabulary of sport, particularly of sports coaches, relies a lot on military analogies and simplistic motivational slogans. There's the classic Andy Townsend line when he's commentating on a football match: 'Who wants it more, Clive?' It's a fair question because often the side that wants to win more than the opposition will do just that. I saw the difference between cricketers who were enjoying themselves and those who were driven when I moved from Northants to Sussex.

Harmy, however, was more complicated. You couldn't just scream slogans at someone like him and expect it to work. It was no good asking him what his processes were and military analogies didn't work either because he found them absurd. On the day he bowled that infamous first ball of the Ashes at the Gabba he went back to his hotel room, switched on the news and heard that two soldiers had died in Afghanistan. No one knew better than Harmy how irrelevant cricket seemed compared to someone losing their life. When someone asks you how much you 'want' it, there's often an implication of cowardice, and I think he resented that more than anything. During one of our running sessions in New Zealand he suddenly started accelerating like he had giraffe legs. We didn't know he packed that kind of pace; he was rapid! In hindsight he was maybe trying to throw himself into it to take his mind off his condition.

Sending Steve home after that first Test would have been an easier decision than dropping Hoggy because even though he was masking the full extent of his issues, it was obvious how unhappy he was. That said, Vaughan wouldn't have been human if he hadn't been affected by this. Why was cricket making so many of his teammates miserable? By then he'd come to the conclusion that Moores was part of the problem for the older guard. Vaughan's mental and emotional sub-circuits were so in tune with Duncan that it must have been like having a car for ten years and suddenly having to get used to a new one.

We turned the New Zealand series around to win 2-1, but I didn't enjoy the tour. A lot of us had stopped enjoying our cricket and I got the feeling I wasn't progressing as much as I wanted to.

We beat New Zealand in the return series that spring, but then lost 2-1 to a much stronger South African side. That was the series that finished off Vaughan, and for the first time, I was getting serious criticism for my bowling from sources other than Duncan Fletcher.

Chapter 22

Guantanamo Cricket

Graeme Smith was the sort of man who could really take the joy out of cricket for a bowler. He wasn't a lot of fun for the fielders either, and he was positively lethal for England captains, seeing off Nasser in 2003, Vaughan in 2008 and Andrew Strauss in 2012.

Smith was a master of Guantanamo cricket. At one point during the 2008 series with his South Africa side I bowled over 450 balls without taking a wicket, and whatever you might say about it in a press conference, that messes with your head.

Bowling against that South African team was like being a rat trapped on a wheel. If Smith didn't score, they had Hashim Amla, AB de Villiers, Ashwell Prince and Jacques Kallis, with Mark Boucher playing the Gilchrist role as an agent of demoralisation down the order.

By the summer of 2008, some of our squad didn't need demoralising, although this was another series that had actually started well, only to enter a tailspin.

In the first Test at Lord's Ian Bell made 199 and KP 152, as we declared on 593-8. I took 4-74 and we got them all out for 247, but in the second innings we entered Cricket Guantanamo. My figures were 60-15-116-0 and Smith, Neil McKenzie and Amla all made centuries on a dead track.

It ended in a sterile draw and by the time we got to Headingley a few days later, their bowling attack had come to life.

There were signs, meanwhile, that English cricket was losing the plot. Behind the scenes the ECB had fallen for 'Sir' Allen Stanford's Super Six Bullshit Extravaganza and had agreed to send a team for a winner takes all $20 million match that November. (And it is amazing just how many apparently sensible people fell for him.)

More pressingly, Ryan Sidebottom had been ruled out of the second Test so the obvious thing to do would have been to call up Graham Onions, or recall either Matthew Hoggard or Steve Harmison. Instead they went for Darren Pattinson.

None of what followed was Darren's fault. He was a nice guy who'd been working as a roof tiler in Australia and was playing grade cricket when he was called up by Victoria. He did well and was recommended to Notts. When he did well there he was called up, even though at the age of twenty-nine he'd only played eleven first class games.

As he'd spent the first six years of his life in Grimsby and only had a British passport, he was arguably better qualified for England than a host of other players, but he spoke with a strong Australian accent, and barely had enough time to learn what was on the ECB's values card before he was pitched into a series against some of the world's greatest batsmen. He actually did OK, taking 2-95 in the first innings, but we ended up losing by ten wickets.

In the second innings they took the single they needed to win off his first ball and that was the end of another international career, almost as soon as it had begun. His selection was so off the cuff the ECB didn't have time to implement the usual 'make him seem English' PR strategy they deployed whenever they selected someone who didn't meet with the full approval of the Peter Oborne sect. There was no time to get a tattoo done, he didn't bat for long enough to be able to kiss his helmet and they didn't have the time to arrange sympathetic interviews with journalists on his love for the mother country because, with Sidebottom fit again, they bombed him out before the third Test at Edgbaston.

At this point we were like the sailors who'd abandoned the USS *Indianapolis*, linking arms in the water and wondering who the sharks were coming for next. This time it was Vaughan. His scores for the series (2 at Lord's, 0 and 21 at Headingley) were low and the pressure was finally getting to him. When Mike Selvey asked him why I wasn't taking responsibility for setting my own fields, he said I could only set 'university' fields. That wasn't the Vaughan I knew: he sounded rattled and defensive, as if he'd run out of ideas.

At Edgbaston he made a first ball duck and a painful 19 in the second innings. It wasn't as one-sided as Headingley because we set them 281 and went into day four thinking we were probably going to win. I got Amla lbw for just 6 and when I had de Villiers caught by Paul Collingwood they still needed over a 100 with five wickets down, but Smith made an unbeaten 154 and Mark Boucher stayed with him until the end.

At that point we had no idea Vaughan was going to quit. We knew he was struggling, but with one Test left we thought he might drop down the order to five or six where the waters were usually calmer.

Instead he called a press conference at Loughborough for the following day and said he was quitting as captain. 'I don't want to become a cynical old man.' he said. 'I want to be the fresh optimistic guy I've always been.'

He also made himself unavailable for the final Test.

It made sense. He'd lost the joy and for the sake of his own mental health he needed to walk away. It takes a hard man to watch someone like Marcus Trescothick disintegrate in front of your eyes and carry on as if nothing's happened. It takes an equally hard man to end the international career of someone like Matthew Hoggard, and the cumulative effect of this, the relentlessness of the training and his own form had ground him down. I had to wonder if the cynicism reference was anything to do with the way Pattinson had been treated.

We needed a new captain, someone who could be as fresh and optimistic as Vaughan once was, while piling on the runs, as Vaughan once had.

They picked the right man. They just picked him at the wrong time.

Chapter 23

Captain Pietersen

In English cricket the captaincy theory goes in cycles. In the late nineties, they decided Nasser should captain the Test side while Adam Hollioake took charge of the one-dayers.

After a while they agreed Vaughan should do both jobs but by 2011, we were in a three-captain phase as Stuart Broad took over the T20 side, Strauss skippered in Test matches and Alastair Cook managed in 50-over cricket.

In 2008, the prevailing wisdom was that we needed a single captain who would unify the Test and limited overs sides. It was also decreed that whoever this was had to be in both teams on merit, which significantly narrowed the selection pool. It narrowed further when Paul Collingwood, who was serving a ban for slow over rates (a hanging offence for some in the *TMS* box), ruled himself out of contention shortly after Vaughan resigned. As Freddie's fitness was questionable and Strauss wasn't an automatic choice for the one-dayers, that left KP.

If the England captain's job had been purely about cricket it might well have worked. As well as being a ludicrously talented batsman he was a decent off-spinner and he absorbed a prodigious amount of cricket knowledge, even if he didn't have any experience as an actual captain. He wasn't, however, anyone's idea of a diplomat. When we were batting against Australia he'd hit a ball to the boundary and yell 'Fetch it, fetch it' at the fielders, as if he were ordering his dog to go after a stick! His political skills also needed some work.

An England captain has to do a lot more than choose the tactics. The ECB might ask him to open a pavilion. They might want him to fluff the sponsors. And they might need to him to shake the hand of a fascist dictator who'd rather starve his people to death than surrender his power.

A geo-political crisis ensnares English cricket at least once a decade, usually, but not exclusively, gestating in the southern part of Africa. If you're particularly unlucky, like Nasser, you might end up being shunted into a line-up and ordered to shake the hand of a tyrant like Robert Mugabe. You might also have to deal with the fallout of a rebel tour. It can't have been much fun being David Gower in 1989 when half his squad was being tapped up behind his back, and Micky Stewart subsequently described Alan Igglesden as England's 'seventeenth-choice' pace bowler. Even during peacetime you might have to mask your contempt for selections you patently disagree with, in precisely the way Mike Atherton couldn't when he was told he had to use Martin McCague instead of Angus Fraser back in 1994.

When it came to the art of pretending to like people you inwardly despised, KP was an amateur in an industry full of professionals.

He was initially made skipper on a temporary basis, but when we thrashed South Africa in both the final Test and the one-day series that followed, the ECB had to give him the job. His first official assignment was to captain a side for a one-off Twenty20 match against a side assembled by a fat American crook who thought he looked like Tom Selleck and actually looked like Jabba the Hutt. It was a step up from meeting Mugabe, I suppose.

I wasn't selected for the Stanford Super Sixes so it's easy for me to sit in judgement, but fuck it, let's do it anyway.

The bounty was $20 million, the concept, winner takes all. No one knew where the money was coming from and too many people couldn't be bothered to ask. It beggars belief that no one had done due diligence on Stanford.

Through no fault of his own, KP's captaincy began in embarrassing circumstances. Yet before the month was out we were all wishing that the worst thing we had to worry about was what a lecherous crook like Stanford was doing on the boundary.

Chapter 24

Bombs in Mumbai

An international cricketer playing all three formats of the game might find himself in hotel rooms for two-thirds of the year.

The quality is variable. If you're playing Pakistan, now that they're exiled to the UAE you might get to stay in the seven-star Emirates Palace, where each room has a butler, there are more swimming pools than you can count and there's a harpist in the lobby.

If you've got a four-day game in Canterbury, you might get a Holiday Inn next to a dual carriageway opposite a Rochester housing estate, where staring at the trouser press is usually more interesting than the Freeview TV.

The extremes in India are even more obvious. India is a hard tour for a number of reasons. The first is the heat. When people ask if I should be used to this because of my Indian heritage, I have to point out I grew up in Stopsley, where we think it's a heatwave if the temperature gets above 20 degrees on consecutive days.

The second is your health: cricketers always worry about getting injured and there's the increased risk of what we might call 'stomach complaints'.

The third is the intensity of the support, which at times makes the Western Terrace at Headingley sound like a croquet match.

And above all, India are a seriously good side. It might be exciting knowing that you're bowling to Tendulkar and Dravid, but that doesn't make it easy to sleep.

At the end of the 2006 tour everyone knew we'd be staying at the Taj Mahal Palace Hotel in Mumbai and it was a real morale boost – luxurious, relaxing, clean and a real haven after a gruelling month of cricket. £300 for a room, and someone else is paying.

We were rejuvenated and it might well have contributed to us squaring that series.

Two years later, I was in Bangalore with the Performance Squad. Michael Vaughan, Andrew Strauss and I were due to fly to Mumbai two days later to meet up with the boys from the one-day squad. Our Test match kit was already at the Taj. Blazers, pads, helmets, caps, ties, the lot, all of it in storage. We were only in Bangalore because our training camp had been switched at the last minute. I still don't know why the venue was moved, but if it hadn't been I might not be writing this story now.

On 26 November, ten members of an Islamic terror group called Lashkar-e-Taiba began a series of attacks at strategic locations in Mumbai, including the Taj Hotel. The siege lasted for four days and the Taj was the site of the terrorists' last stand. On the first day a bomb went off in the lobby we'd all used. Two bombs went off in the lifts we'd all used. Three went off in the restaurant we'd all used. Gunmen started spraying the hotel with bullets.

That night, firefighters managed to rescue 200 hostages using ladders, but there were still a handful of hostages being held in a room and by the time the authorities had neutralised the attackers, thirty-one people had been murdered.

In all, 166 people were killed and 293 wounded during the attacks. We watched it on TV in our hotel in Bangalore in a state of disbelief and horror.

A lot of people assumed we were in the hotel because they didn't realise we'd moved to Bangalore. Friends and family want to know if you're OK. The media want to know how you feel – a subtle difference.

How do you feel? Numb. Shocked. Horrified. Disbelieving. You sit there wondering if the staff who served your food, cleaned your room or smiled at you in the lift are dead. You wonder how you'd have reacted. You remember the room you stayed in and try to work out if you could have barricaded yourself in. As England cricketers, would we have been targets? As a Sikh playing for England, would I have been more or less likely to get shot?

At some point the shock fades and it occurs to you that as cricketers you will still be expected to play cricket. The British government want you to 'Keep calm and carry on'. They may have a point. The 2005 Ashes series started just a fortnight after the 7-7 bombings in London. The bombers travelled to London from Luton station, my home town. Should I have stopped using the Luton to London train, or travelling on the Tube? No, but I'll be honest and say that in the immediate aftermath of the Mumbai attacks I just wanted to go home and stay there.

I changed my mind when our security chief, Reg Dickason, told me it was safe to go back.

Reg was our Jack Bauer. As a policeman he'd worked on covert anti-drug trafficking operations and had run into the Mafia. You didn't take on that kind of work unless you had balls made of titanium. He was a man mountain, with massive upper arms, tattoos and a goatee beard. Reg was an honorary squad member. He'd even join in training sessions, standing there with pads on his hands as we laced up with boxing gloves and tried to hit him as hard as we could. I doubt he even felt the blows.

Most importantly, he didn't bullshit us. We went to a holding camp (OK, a luxury hotel) in Abu Dhabi where the ECB tried to convince the squad we needed to complete the tour.

It wasn't the usual sales pitch. They called us to a meeting room and sat us in front of a white board where Reg told us what might happen.

'They might try and attack us here, here and here … if they attack here, like this, this many people will die … if they do this, here, this many people will die …'

KP said it was like trying to work out a Duckworth Lewis calculation for your own life.

Having said all this, Reg then gave us his professional opinion. With the measures taken by the Indian security forces, we would be OK. He'd dealt with high-profile politicians and high-net-worth individuals who were at risk of kidnappings. You can never eliminate risk entirely, but that applies when you're crossing the road. In his assessment we were OK.

That was good enough for me, but some, if not most, of the squad needed more convincing. KP was on the phone for every waking hour trying to convince them. We didn't have kids so it was an easier decision for us than it was for them and I didn't blame any of them for having doubts, but I also had an additional motive for going back.

This Test match was going to be an act of defiance for the whole of India. They were uniting and showing they'd survived. The cricket was going to be a celebration and for me it was an opportunity to be a hero. I was already dreaming of being the Sikh that won the first Test match in India after the attacks.

The Indian crowds had always been brilliant with me, even though I was playing for England. They took pride in my achievements and in my mind I was thinking if I could star in this match I'd become a legend.

The game proved pivotal for my career, but not in the way I'd hoped.

***

It the Scorsese-directed biopic of my life, this is the scene where I feel like I'm in a war film. From the moment we got off the plane we were flanked by soldiers in camouflage gear and peaked caps, although even with their hats on, KP was at least a foot taller than his guards. They strutted through the airport, flanked by armed regular army soldiers in classic khaki, separating us from around a thousand fans who thought we were heroes just for turning up.

They'd assigned 3,000 police officers to protect us. We had men on every floor of the hotel, commandos all over the city and the stadium itself was like the Green Zone in Baghdad.

Sachin later said the sacrifices the security forces made inspired them to victory. For me personally, it was a weird feeling, because the country of my parents and my ancestors was poised for this outpouring of joy and relief, and I was trying to hijack the moment.

It was set up exactly according to the script. Or at least, my script. I took out VVS Laxman, MS Dhoni and Harbhajan Singh in the first innings and we led by 75. We declared on 311-9 in the second innings, setting them a record target. This was the moment where I should have spun England to a historic victory and staked my claim as The Greatest Spin Bowler in the World, but I stalled. By the end of the innings you could argue I wasn't even the best spinner in the team.

I think Graeme Swann was a bit more intelligent than me at understanding his cricket. He would challenge himself and say, 'I'm not just going to bowl two an over and wait for the batsmen to make a mistake.' He would change his dip, his loop, and his foot settings, and that type of cricket only really happened for me when I went to Sussex.

India worked us for singles, picking us off a ball at a time and keeping the scoreboard moving so we couldn't build any pressure.

Sachin and Yuvraj Singh kept their pads well inside the line, negating the risk of lbw. I went over the wicket, aimed at the rough and nothing happened, all day.

Sachin paddled Swanny for 4 to bring up his century and score the winning runs with the same blow. The sub-continent erupted with joy, and as a human being and knowing what they'd been through, a part of me had to feel happy for them. As a human being, a part of me also felt envy. When I saw my hero being feted as a demigod, I was thinking, 'That could have been me.'

We drew the second Test. Losing a series 1-0 to world-class opponents, in circumstances like these, isn't terrible, but behind the scenes things were coming to a head with Moores and KP. The latter offered to resign because he said he couldn't work with Moores any more. It felt like a bluff, but the ECB called it and got rid of them both.

The man they should have made captain in the first place, Andrew Strauss, took over. KP should have been Strauss's vice-captain. He was a very passionate guy, but I just felt that he was such a big player and raw talent that maybe he should have hung back a bit. He could have learned the ropes and watched Strauss and how he handled the politics.

KP just loved batting. When we played together in the nets it was nearly as competitive as when I played my mini-Ashes series with Huss. He was a hard training partner, but I know he respected the bowling I used to give him.

I think to him it doesn't really matter if he's liked or not. He knew he was one of the superstars of the game, getting work, and playing in all the big leagues. Some people want to be liked, some people think, 'Who cares?'

Ultimately, when I left Sussex a few years later, under something of a cloud, he was one of the first people to text me with his support. He hadn't forgotten me and at times like that, knowing you haven't been forgotten means more than you can say.

Chapter 25

Dunkirk

We somehow lost our next series in the West Indies 1-0, where Swanny took nineteen wickets at an average of 24.05 and I took five at 54.00.

On that form I couldn't complain about being left out of the team for the return series with the West Indies in May. I also sat out the standard group stage humiliation in the World Twenty20 but I was back for the first Ashes Test in Cardiff. It was my last ever home Test match.

There comes a point as a bowler when it seems as if nothing you try makes a difference. I'd felt it against Graeme Smith and the South Africans the year before and I'd felt it again bowling to Sachin in Chennai.

We'd reached that point and gone well beyond it on the Saturday of the Cardiff Test. Four of the Australians made centuries. I bowled Ricky Ponting, but by then he'd already hit 150 and that was my only wicket from thirty-five overs. We were back in Cricket Guantanamo and today's lesson was in the ancient Australian art of mental disintegration. They were deliberately trying to break us, and it was working.

Ponting was playing me too easily. So was Michael Clarke. As I ran in to bowl to them I knew that unless something drastic happened this was going to be my last Test for a while. Swanny's position was no longer up for grabs. I'd been selected ahead of Graham Onions and as unhelpful as the track was, I wasn't doing anything to justify that selection.

By the time they'd declared during the afternoon session they'd reached 674-6. The deficit, 239, was manageable, but everyone knew our chances were meagre.

Inevitably you look around the dressing room and wonder who's going to make the contributions you need. Alastair Cook, a classic 'company man', to use KP's back-handed compliment, was precisely the kind of batsman you'd look to in this kind of situation, but he lasted just twelve balls before he was lbw to Mitchell Johnson.

Ravi Bopara, a stylish and aggressive player but not a natural blocker, made a single before Hilfenhaus got him lbw to the third ball he'd faced.

Strauss and KP dragged us to 20-2 at tea, but during the interval it began to rain. Heavily.

The entire evening session was wiped out, which at least gave us hope we might be able to bat out the final day, even if we'd have to face an increased number of overs.

The forecast for the Sunday, however, didn't offer any encouragement. We knew we'd have to survive three extended sessions, or erode their lead to the point we'd make them bat again.

Colly fronted up for the press conference on the Saturday night. He knew the script: honesty, realism, defiance. The press liked Colly. Everyone did. We'd all had our ECB media training and that was all they wanted you to say in a situation like this. Feed the journalists a few lines about fat ladies singing and it not being over till it's over, and they go away happy, or if not happy, then at least sated.

There was a difference between what we could say in public and what we were feeling privately, and the fighting-till-the-end speech sounded better coming from Colly, because he sounded like he believed it.

Defeatism is like a cancer in any dressing room and no one thought we were beaten at the end of day four, but we were realistic. Behind the scenes some of the team were struggling. KP was suffering physically as well as mentally, having an epidural for his Achilles injury. Swanny, who always tried to lighten the mood, was saying that we'd at least be able to get home early, but I probably knew him better than anyone else in the team and saw through the gallows humour. It was a joke to mask the pain he felt for bowling, in his own words, 'like an absolute idiot', although he had at least made 47 not out in the first innings.

I personally knew that we had no chance of winning and thought our chances of getting a draw were worse than fifty-fifty, but I'd seen and read enough about the history of the game to know we still stood a chance of writing another chapter.

I'd watched Mike Atherton make 185 not out against South Africa in Johannesburg, when he'd batted for over ten hours to save the Test match. That was arguably the greatest innings of a great career. I'd also seen Brett Lee and Glenn McGrath save the third Test at Old Trafford four years previously and remembered how they'd celebrated as if they'd won the World Cup.

What I didn't know was that I was about to be involved in a finish that more than one commentator would liken to Dunkirk. Nor did I have any idea how uncomfortably that analogy would work out for me personally.

***

KP was the first man to go on Sunday morning and his obituaries had been written well in advance. The press boys, particularly some of the English writers, absolutely hated him, with a level of venom I never understood. The Aussies also slated him for supposedly being South African, although how they could claim the moral high ground with a team entirely devoid of Aboriginals was unclear.

'That's the way I play,' was the line that would always haunt Kevin. It did him a disservice because he was so talented he could play any way he liked, but he'd been hammered for his first innings dismissal when he'd played a reckless shot to Nathan Hauritz and been caught by Simon Katich.

This time around he was being cautious, but he maybe overdid it because he misread a delivery from Hilfenhaus that he expected to turn. He left it, thinking it would miss the stumps, but it clipped off.

Geoff Boycott said he was 'like a spoilt child, the family favourite who can get away with anything because he is the golden boy'. If anything, the reverse was true.

It was the sort of mistake that could have happened at any time during any of his greatest innings, but the mob wanted a scapegoat rather than a philosopher and KP was always going to get more of the blame than Andrew Strauss for example, the next man to fall.

Straussy was another great company man, destined for high office from early in his career, but he was caught behind for 17 after facing fifty-four balls, trying a cut shot. Boycs criticised him too, though only for his apparent failure to tell KP off in a sufficiently graphic, public way.

His dismissal brought in Matt Prior, the man KP later called 'Le Grand Fromage' in his book. Again, I didn't get the criticism. In a team game, why can't everyone make the effort to get along? Matty was another player you'd want alongside you in a situation like this, arguably the wicketkeeping all-rounder we'd been looking for since Alec Stewart. He was an excellent cutter but he was tricked by a ball from Hauritz that bounced more than he thought it would and caught by Michael Clarke at slip. He lasted thirty-four balls. By now we were five down and in deep trouble, although as long as Paul Collingwood was there, there was always hope.

Colly was like a barnacle, and with Freddie at the other end, the equation changed.

I went from thinking I'd probably just have to play a cameo innings to wondering if I'd need to bat at all. By the time Johnson had Freddie caught by Ponting at second slip, they'd batted for twenty-three overs and the match situation had altered significantly.

Something weird was happening around the ground. It was the first Test match ever to be staged in Cardiff and we really didn't know how the fans would take to us. If the England rugby team had been playing across the road at the Millennium Stadium, the home crowd would have been baying for English blood, but at cricket they wanted us to win.

Alec Stewart could never get his head around the idea that Robert Croft could play for England but support Wales at rugby. When Crofty helped save a Test for England against South Africa in 1998, in the post-match interview Stewie said, 'Little Robert Croft proved he's English today!'

That was the kind of spirit we were now trying to harness and the crowd was reacting. They were English for the day.

At one point we even got some unexpected help from a pitch invasion: two men evaded security and unfurled a banner protesting about Ryan Air. One of them later said he'd done it because the airline had sacked his daughter the night before. The only thing that surprised me about this was that no one from the Australian media suggested that Michael O'Leary had fired her on purpose.

The problem was that every time the odds seemed to tilt slightly back in favour, we'd lose a wicket. Stuart Broad hung in there for a full hour before he was lbw to Hauritz. Swanny lasted even longer and crucially he made 31 while he was doing it, but he was lbw to Hilfenhaus, exposing the tail.

From my point of view, it was the cue to pad up. And it was now that the nervous system really started to go into overdrive. It's almost always the same when you're waiting to go in. The heart rate soars. Your temples throb. You sweat and need to go to the toilet every few minutes. The only situations in which you don't get nervous are when your team already has a huge total on the board and you're going to have a bit of a slog to score a few quick runs, or if the game's effectively up and the pressure's off.

I was now in a situation where, for the first time in my life, I was one ball away from having to bat to save an Ashes Test match and the only way to relieve the tension was to get out in the middle. Ashley Giles will tell you the same thing about the Trent Bridge Test in 2005. Once you get out there, the tension melts away. It's liberating.

The problem was I thought I'd be partnering Colly, who'd shield me from the strike. Instead, after 245 balls and 344 minutes, Colly hit Peter Siddle to gully and he was caught by Mike Hussey, who nearly dropped him, but gathered the ball at the second attempt.

The most unforgettable hour of my entire life was about to begin.

***

The Australians had apparently been delighted when they heard Jimmy Anderson had been selected on the Wednesday morning. Justin Langer's scouting report described him as 'a bit of a pussy' and this was 'accidentally' leaked to the Australian media, but it backfired on the Australians because it riled us.

Jimmy wasn't a specialist, but he could hang around. So could I. I was once described by *The Guardian* as 'arguably the worst batsman in Test cricket'. That was bullshit. Ten years earlier, England had a tail of Alan Mullally, Devon Malcolm, Phil Tufnell and Ed Giddins, four batsmen who might yield ten runs between them if you were lucky. Tuffers in particular had never bought into the idea that the lower order needed to contribute. His retort was that the batsmen should try to help him bowl against Brian Lara, but Duncan Fletcher knew that if a tail-ender could hang around for even half an hour, it could be the difference between winning and losing – or, in this case, drawing. As part of his master plan for English cricket all the specialist bowlers were allocated 'batting buddies' to help them. Colly was mine, and over the next hour I banished the idea that I was a rabbit.

You can see me smiling as I went in. I knew the Australians thought they were 99 per cent certain to win. If we lost, the venom was going to be sprayed all over Straussy for his team selection or KP for being KP, but no one was going to blame the so-called worst batsman in the world. And above it all, cricket is supposed to be fun. If you play in a game like this, cricket *is* fun; it's worth all the hours you spend toiling in a field and all the ridicule you endure to be involved in a finish that people will talk about for the rest of their lives.

If I'd been facing McGrath and Warne, I might have been less nonchalant, but they'd retired. Peter Siddle and Nathan Hauritz were both very good bowlers, but they couldn't panic you into a dismissal. Hauritz was baby-faced, but he wasn't an assassin, whilst Siddle was wearing the kind of beady necklace you'd normally see on a student at Glastonbury.

Maybe the strangest thing of all was how, out in the middle, no one seemed to know exactly what we needed to do to secure the draw. What we did know was that reducing the number of deliveries we'd have to face during that time would obviously increase our chances of surviving.

When I went in there were 11.3 overs left, but we were only 6 runs behind. If we could chalk those off Australia would need to bat again, which would wipe ten minutes (and two overs) off the clock for the change of innings.

The atmosphere was like nothing I'd experienced before, or am ever likely to experience again. It veered between raucous and silent, and the closest thing I can compare it to is a penalty shootout in a World Cup. Every time we blocked a ball the noise was deafening, but only for a few seconds as the crowd realised the next delivery was imminent and it might all be over.

The Australians appealed like Colombian footballers and every time they were turned down, a crescendo of jeering would rise from the Anglo–Welsh in the stands.

Between overs the Welsh fans were singing *Bread of Heaven* and *You're Not Singing Any More* at the Australians, but the biggest roar came when Jimmy squeezed one past the slips for 4, meaning they'd have to bat again.

Confusion was starting to reign out in the middle. What we didn't know was that by 6.41 pm, whatever happened, the game would be declared over, so the twelfth man, Bilal Shafayat, was sent out with a new pair of gloves for Jimmy and to deliver the message.

Ponting was irate and told him to 'get off the fucking field'. He later described it as 'ordinary' behaviour and we all knew what he meant, but every honest Australian player will tell you they would have been doing exactly the same thing in that situation, just as every honest English player would admit to being outraged if they'd been on the receiving end.

The language deteriorated. Jimmy took a drink and spilled some on his gloves. He started to wring his hands to get them dry and the dressing room thought he was signalling for an injury, so our physio Steve McCaig went on to see if he was all right.

Ponting erupted. 'What the fuck are you doing on here, you fat cunt!'

Steve, an Australian who'd regarded Ponting as one of his heroes, was so crushed by the abuse he couldn't celebrate with us afterwards. I'm told that Brian Woolnough of the *Star* declared it was 'embarrassing' to anyone who'd listened in the press box. (The following morning, the front page of Brian's paper carried the headline 'Jacko's Killers Unveiled!', while on the inside pages they said 7 million migrants were heading to Britain, 'teens should have sex to stay healthy' and 'Pete begged me for a threesome'. Perhaps self-awareness wasn't Brian's strong point.)

From the moment we'd edged in front we were in a kind of no-man's-land. The simplicity of the equation had changed. Now we knew if we got out the game wouldn't automatically end, but there was still a risk that if we fell too early, they'd be able to knock off the runs.

This actually complicated things. The more we score, the more they have to chase, so should we try to add a few runs? In the confusion we stupidly went for a single and I had to dive to make my ground, getting a face full of Welsh soil.

Ponting's final ruse was to bring on Marcus North, the kind of occasional bowler who can make you subconsciously drop your guard. Jimmy hit his first delivery square of the wicket but into the air. It landed safely and we went through for a single. When I hit his next ball for 4, the Australians seemed to give up, although I didn't know we were definitely safe until the umpires removed the bails three overs later.

***

More than one commentator made the comparison with Dunkirk. It wasn't a victory, but without it we would have almost certainly have lost the Ashes. Yet as with Dunkirk, there were people left on the beach. And when the euphoria had subsided, I learned I was one of them. I didn't play for England for another three years.

Chapter 26

Montage (Part 1)

In the Scorsese-directed biopic of my life, this is where the first montage comes in, condensing a series of grim events that unfolded over several months into one, sixty-second sequence. I lose my place in the England team. Well that's OK; I'll just go back to Northants, take a sackful of wickets and get my place back. I've still got a central contract, right? I took eighteen wickets from thirteen games. Well OK, I'll learn from it and be better next season.

Except at the end of the season, I lose my central contract.

Not to worry, my agency, Paragon, specialists in talent management, will sort me out with a new deal, right? Wrong. They drop me. Evidently I was one talent they no longer felt they could manage.

Then I get called into the office at Wantage Road and told they're letting me go. In the same office where I once told Steve Coverdale that I wanted to be The Greatest Spin Bowler in the World, I was now being told I wasn't even The Greatest Spinner in Northants.

David Capel delivered the news. Even though Graeme White, who'd been pushing me all season, was off to Notts, they were going with Nicky Boje and the Kolpak players. I think it was around this time that my views on Kolpak players may have evolved slightly.

Northants thought I was going to get an ECB contract and had budgeted accordingly. They'd also changed the pitches at Wantage Road. Bunsens were out, pace and bounce was in.

I knew other clubs were interested, but I wanted to stay. I should never have left Northants; it felt like my home and if I'd stayed in that environment my issues might never have happened. They just didn't want me enough. Or at all.

I could handle being left out of the side for Graeme Swann, Ashley Giles or Graham Onions. But Nicky Boje?

Northants didn't give me much of a send-off. In my last game we absolutely thrashed Surrey. I wrapped up their innings by getting Pedro Collins stumped by Niall O'Brien and watched as we ticked off the runs in under sixteen overs.

I remember going up to Capes and saying, 'Mate, I grew up here, under you. I came to talk to you when I wanted to learn about cricket, I played for England and now I need your backing to stay at Northants because I'm still a homegrown player and you're backing the Kolpak players! Why would you bring Kolpak players into the English game? Where's the long-term interest? What happens to homegrown players?'

It didn't work. I even offered to take a pay cut. They just weren't interested.

As a parting gift I left Northants with £10,000 of my own money to show there were no hard feelings, although in reality I can't pretend it didn't hurt, because it did.

I can't pretend I wasn't angry, because I was, but as I'm writing this I've just heard David Capel has had successful surgery for a brain tumour. Time has healed the wound to a large extent and any lingering resentment I may have felt towards Capes dissolved as soon as I heard the news.

***

Then I got married. That lasted for about six months. That was my fault.

I was never a ladies' man, nor a playboy. I didn't really get a lot of attention, and when I got married I hadn't had a proper relationship or anything like that, like where you live together and for two to three years you're in each other's pockets and the woman starts hating it because the man takes his socks off and leaves them on the floor.

I didn't experience that level of closeness because I was so busy with the cricket and also my studies.

It's not that I wasn't interested. I'm not going to name anybody, but when I went to Bedford Modern I might get on a different bus if a girl I liked was on it. If my mates were talking to some nice girls you'd find a reason to go and speak to them. There were hidden, subtle ways of trying to introduce yourself but at the same time, my cricket still was growing, it wasn't stopping. My mentor at the time, Dave Parsooth, said if you want to go into that world, cricket won't happen, so I was always cautious.

Dave said you've got to focus on one thing. Then your energy only goes into one thing, otherwise it could distract you and stop you getting to your destination. He said you're so young, there's time for these things later in life. In a way he was right, because I made my debut when I was twenty-three.

I met Gursharan through friends. I don't remember where, but we were in the same social circle and after a while it developed into something more.

We didn't live together though, and maybe we should have. Marriage was something we seemed to drift into. Dave told me he didn't think I was ready and after all these years, I have to admit I wasn't mature enough for a relationship. When my sister got married a few years later, I realised what it all meant, how it worked and what you needed to do to make it work.

At the time I should have said let's wait six months to see where we are, but I didn't.

There were 700 people at our wedding: that's more than you get for some county championship matches, although it wasn't unusual for a Sikh wedding. It was also the first wedding for this generation in our respective families, so it was always going to be a big celebration.

In the Punjabi culture we don't do things by half measures so we had an English-style stag do with Punjabi-level partying. There were about fifty of my mates there – from school, from Luton Indians, from our temple – and we had a great time.

We got married in the Sikh temple in Coventry. We had little messenger girls and I can remember asking one of them to go to Gursharan and tell her, 'Don't be nervous.'

In the Sikh culture people think you shouldn't live together before you get married, but so many people end up getting divorced. You should know each other's habits, and if you get the chance to live together you should take it, because the UK divorce rate is 42 per cent.

My sister didn't live with her husband before their wedding and her marriage is successful, so it can work, but I'm older now and I've got to get this decision right second time around. I've got friends who've had two divorces, even at my age, and I'm thinking, 'Damn, man, I don't want to be in their position.' Even in India, people are fifty-five and getting divorced even after twenty-five years of marriage. They think, 'I've raised the children and I'm actually bored of you, I want to move on now. I've raised them, you're financially OK, I'll give you a bit of a payout, that's it. I can move on now with my other life.'

My mum always thought I didn't know how to interact with the rest of the family because I'd always been playing cricket instead of attending family functions. Now I had two families I didn't know how to interact with! The cricket lifestyle doesn't help your chances of a successful marriage. We just didn't get the chance to spend time together.

I was going to Australia, to play cricket, and I can remember speaking to Neil Burns and saying, 'Do you know what? I'm not sure what to do about my marriage.'

He said, 'Why don't you both go to Australia, neutral ground, no friends and family, you play your cricket, she can have a three-month holiday?' I think on the day we were due to go, she refused.

I just felt that in that relationship, whenever we were close to making things happen, they didn't. On the day before we were supposed to be going to Australia, we had the tickets and everything arranged and she didn't want to go.

Things kept happening like that and after a while you think, maybe it's just destiny? Whenever we tried to reconcile, it fell through, and it got to a point where I thought, 'Maybe this is it.' You just think perhaps we're two human beings who are not meant to be together.

Throughout the marriage this was a consistent pattern. We'd make a plan, agree to make it work and never follow through. We had a bit of a break; she did some travelling in India and some charity work while I was in Australia, and it was just one of those relationships. After a while we got divorced. It was nobody's fault but mine.

**

I wasn't the kind of cricketer who got groupies, but years later, I met a woman with a very forceful personality and a really strong accent. I wasn't sure how old she was, maybe in her late forties or early fifties, and she sounded either Eastern European or Russian. When I met her she grinned at me and said, 'I have devoted my entiiiiiire liiiiife to the pursuit of plaaay-sure.'

I thought, 'Is she coming on to me?' I wasn't sure, but something about her put me off. I can remember thinking to myself, 'If I get involved here I think I'm going to end up getting fed to the fucking pigs.'

At the time of writing, I'm still single.

Chapter 27

Good Old Sussex by the Sea

I wasn't done with cricket by a long way but at twenty-seven years of age, I needed a new club.

Warwickshire were interested and it would have been handy for the Sikh Temple in Coventry where we had a lot of friends, but in the end I fancied joining Sussex, even though they were in Division Two.

It was full of cricketers who knew how to win matches, as opposed to Northants, which was a collection of talented players who didn't know how to finish off their opponents and kept finding ways to lose.

Michael Yardy was the kind of born winner I wanted to play alongside. A fighter. He'd been my roommate on the England A tour and he was one of many reasons why I fancied moving to Hove. The main one was that they wanted me, but there were a lot of other attractions. Brighton was like a little London, full of celebrities like Steve Coogan, Paul McCartney and Norman Cook.

It was very different to Luton and Northants in that there wasn't a huge Sikh community there, but it was a diverse, tolerant place where you could live your life without anyone bothering you. For a while, at least.

The way that my time at Sussex ended has overshadowed everything else I did there. It was a bit like Steve Coogan's line about the *Titanic*: there were over a thousand miles of very pleasurable sailing before it hit the iceberg.

We, and later I, lived in a two-bedroom flat in the cricketers' ghetto, right by the ground, off Eaton Road. If it hadn't been for all the cricketers in the area I think the average age would have been somewhere in the nineties. It was the sort of neighbourhood where you stood a fifty-fifty chance of getting run over by a mobility scooter every time you went for a pint of milk.

Yards recommended me to the coach, Mark Robinson, and I don't think they could believe their luck that I'd become available.

It took me a while to get going. I was distracted by the state of my marriage, but I eventually took fifty-two wickets in the county championship that summer and all the while I knew I was only ever one Graeme Swann injury away from a recall to the Test lineup.

We won the Division Two title with Yards as captain … and by now you know the drill. He was one of the last people you ever imagined might suffer from mental illness. After Freddie and Marcus.

Yards was a great cricketer, who was brilliant at what he did. He didn't have the natural talent of a Warne or a Pietersen, but his work ethic and sheer determination turned him into a World Cup winner. We had a lot more in common than either of us knew at the time and if anything, of all the players to have suffered with mental health issues in recent years, his case would prove to be the closest to my own.

Later in my career I'd develop a reputation for being introverted and staying in my room a lot when we were on tour. When I was on the Lions Tour with Yards, it was the exact opposite. I couldn't stay in all the time and I'd be saying, 'Come on, let's go out, let's do stuff.' I could see he preferred his home comforts. He'd Facetime his wife and kids, and he loved his room service. This wasn't that unusual for a family man, but I later realised that staying in your hotel room on tour is a classic warning sign.

Yards was suffering in silence, but when Marcus's book came out it gave him the courage he needed to talk to Mark Robinson and tell him something was wrong. I felt sorry for him when he admitted he was suffering, but because of my immaturity, part of me also felt strangely annoyed with myself. Why was I only finding this out when everyone else did? Why didn't I have the people skills to notice something was wrong? Why didn't he come and speak to me?

I can trace the roots of my own paranoia back to this period. The introvert tag was beginning to stick to me at Sussex. Most of the squad had grown up together and they had years of shared experiences that I hadn't been a part of. I was brought in as an established international and expected to perform as such.

I was still England's second choice spinner, but when we went to Australia for the 2010–11 Ashes, I knew I'd only play if Swanny got injured or in the unlikely event the Aussies prepared a raging Bunsen.

The highlight of that winter came during the tour match with Australia A, when Ed Cowan pulled Tim Bresnan to midwicket, where I just happened to be lurking like a panther poised to leap on a gazelle. I leapt to my right like Manuel Neuer and plucked it out of the air with one hand. Never in any doubt.

For the rest of that tour I felt a bit like a net bowler. The first few games were all right but as the tour evolves you just think, what am I doing here? You don't feel part of the XI and as time goes by you feel more and more distance from the players who are starting.

It is difficult. You do train and you have to get involved with doing the drinks, but after a while you get bored with doing that, and the feeling you're nothing more than a net bowler grows. You're in a role of giving, serving for the team, but it's like when we go to the temple and do voluntary service. That was quite a big part of my upbringing. You have to change your mindset, you think, 'I'm serving here for the team, I'm a volunteer,' although obviously they pay you for the tour. It becomes more of a giving role, but that's something as a cricketer you just have to understand.

Some games you play, some you don't. You've got to have the mentality of being a good team man when you're not playing.

It's a lot easier when the team's winning. Even though I didn't play in a single Test, I enjoyed that tour more than either of the other Ashes trips I went on, because it was a brilliant experience to be a part of a squad that had finally won in Australia. I was out there doing the sprinkler dance with everyone else after the final Test.

I also knew that as happy as I was, drinking other people's champagne was never going to be enough for me personally when I hadn't felt like I'd contributed.

＊＊＊

The upshot of it all was that I began getting upset with myself. When Yards came home early from the World Cup a few weeks later, I took it personally: here was my captain coming home from a World Cup and I hadn't even noticed the intense pressure he was under. I was a senior professional now, not a naive rookie on a tour. What kind of a teammate was I if I hadn't even noticed he was suffering?

I'd been watching the games on TV and thinking to myself, 'I can do better than that,' when he came on to bowl. Then I'd check myself. Yes, of course I can bowl better than that, but Yards can bat. And he can catch. He helped us win the World T20 in 2010 and I was not only delighted for him, I was proud, because he was representing us, Sussex, our team. I didn't resent him, but I was starting to resent myself because I wasn't getting a look in at white ball cricket.

I had a huge desire to play one-day and T20 cricket for England. To do that I needed to be playing for Sussex in all forms of the game, and when I didn't get picked I stopped being such a good team man. Why weren't they playing Swanny as a specialist batsman? Then I could be the spinner. This is the sub-continent, for fuck's sake, why aren't you even looking at me?

When I was in the England team, playing and taking wickets, I was happy enough. I was the leading wicket-taker in our series with Pakistan in the UAE, even though they left me out of the first Test.

When I came back for the second Test in Abu Dhabi, I'd been out of the team for three years, but I took 6-62 in their second innings as they set us a target of 145. We still somehow managed to lose by 72 runs. I did well again in the dead third Test in Dubai, taking 2-25 and 5-124, but we were thrashed again to complete a series whitewash.

After an indifferent first Test in the subsequent tour to Sri Lanka, I was out again. I didn't get a look-in that summer, so I went back to Sussex and took fifty-three wickets. They'd built the team around me, but the problem was, I was becoming less and less nice to be around.

Ironically my teammates began to fear my reaction if they dropped catches off my bowling. In the past I used to think, 'OK, I'll just create another chance,' but I was starting to think, 'You fuckers are doing this deliberately.'

That was a symptom of my growing condition: paranoia. It started after I came back from a tour. I went to the gym at Hove, wearing a black puffa jacket I'd bought while I'd been away. I thought it looked the business. As I strolled in, the first person I saw was Yards. He smiled, we exchanged hellos and then he looked at my jacket and said, 'Wow, you look like a footballer!'

It was the kind of innocuous remark you might hear a thousand times a season in a county dressing room, but for some reason it stuck in my head. As I was pounding away at the weights I heard a voice in my head. Not a soft, soothing voice, but an angry, divisive and spiteful one, like Don Logan, the Ben Kingsley character in the film *Sexy Beast*.

'Yards was just taking the piss out of you, Monty.'

'You what?'

'Yards. He was taking the piss out of your jacket. Saying it made you look a right c**t.'

'No he wasn't!'

'He fucking was.'

'Don't be ridiculous. He was just being friendly. He was pleased to see me.'

'Bollocks was he. He said you looked like a right c**t.'

'Shut up!'

The irony here was that if anyone could have related to what I was about go through, it was Yards. He'd been playing grade cricket in Australia during an English winter when he became convinced his house was about to be attacked. He stayed up all night and eventually had to move to alternative accommodation.

He had to manage his condition. It worked for a while, but by 2012 he'd effectively given up on the idea of playing for England. At one point he was suffering from delusions. He'd been on a night out with the boys in Brighton, had a few drinks and gone home without incident, but the following day he became convinced he'd physically attacked someone and possibly even killed them. The delusion was so powerful he was considering turning himself in to the police and confessing to something that had only ever happened in his head.

In the end his wife had to convince him that if he really had murdered someone, the police would have been looking for a killer, and in a city like Brighton, full of CCTV cameras, they wouldn't have had any trouble finding him.

Chapter 28

The Greatest Spin Bowler in the World (Part 2)

My inner Don Logan wasn't going to stay buried forever, but I managed to keep him quiet for a while. I was in a good place when we went to India that winter and bowling as well as I had since the onset of Monty Mania.

A lot of the credit for that has to go to Neil Burns. I was relying more and more on him and he gave me these specialist drills before I went on the tour. I'd do intense, physical exercise, and then I'd bowl an over and repeat. I think Burnsy was good at producing intense, fighting cricketers and it really benefited me. Training under exhaustion like this was really enjoyable because it incorporated bowling, and by the time I got to India, I felt great.

Mike Selvey even wrote a piece in *The Guardian* saying that I'd been transformed from a misfit into a dominant personality. That's what bowling Sachin Tendulkar does for you, I suppose. It was almost becoming standard. The Prince of India, who'd written 'Never again!' on the ball I got him out with back in 2006, had become my bunny.

Well, almost …

We won the series 2-1 and I took seventeen wickets from three matches, second only to Swanny, who took twenty and played in all four Tests.

Once again I seemed to have become a better player by omission. They left me out for the first Test and got beaten by nine wickets. There was an outcry in the media when I was excluded – the first time I'd managed to generate that level of outrage since the Brisbane Test in 2006.

Back by popular demand for the second Test in Mumbai, I bowled Virender Sehwag early on, a full delivery that flicked his pads on the way to the stumps.

Then I took Sachin for an encore.

In the great man's own words, this is what happened:

This time the ball came on with the arm while I played for turn. Gautam Gambhir was batting at the other end and at the end of the day's play, he told me that, as I was walking back to the pavilion, Monty had said to Gautam, '*Ball apne aap seedha nikal gaya!*'

For the non-Hindi speakers among you, that translates as: 'The delivery went straight on its own!'

Next up was Virat Kohli. Tempt him with the wide one, watch him drive and there's Nick Compton at cover, diving to his right. By now I'm PUMPED.

Kohli not a big enough wicket for you? How about some MS Dhoni? Tempt him forwards, make the ball jump at him, off the shoulder of the bat and into the diving hands of Swanny at gully.

Who's next? Ashwin? Soften him up with the variations. A loopy one, a full one, a straight one. Make sure his head's spinning then whip in the arm ball Duncan Fletcher said I didn't have. You are PLUMB my friend. *Au revoir. Bonjour Michelle,* five-for, *comment-allez-vous?*

I left Swanny the tailenders. It seemed only fair.

They were all out for 327 and we wobbled a bit at 68-2, but Cookie made 122 and KP, in his redemption Test, hit 186 runs in an innings worthy of a demigod.

The lead was 89. Time for The Greatest Spin Bowler in the World to do his thing, I suppose.

Sehwag, take two. Try the length ball this time, tempt him forwards, tickle his outside edge and leave the rest to Swanny. *Auf wiedersehen.*

Next! Sachin. Again? Well, if I must. Push him back with a straighter ball that doesn't turn. Wait for it to hit the pad. *Au revoir.*

Yuvraj Singh. Tempt him down the track, spin it into him, nibble his glove and Jonny Bairstow can take it at short leg.

Dhoni, take two. Time for an old-fashioned spinner's wicket. Land it on off, turn it away, tickle the edge and let Jonathan Trott gobble it up in the slips. *Ciao.*

Ashwin, part *deux*. Float it up. He can't resist floaters. Drives it to cover and Samit Patel brings it in. *Adios.*

Zaheer Khan. This won't take long, he hasn't got the patience. Holds out for a while and then tries to slog me against the turn. It gets a huge top edge and Matty Prior takes an easy catch. *Do svidaniya,* baby.

England win by ten wickets. I take match figures of 11-210. How do you like me now?

Chapter 29

The Fall

If I could have played one Test match thirty-three times, I'd have picked that one in Mumbai. I was near the summit of the mountain I'd always wanted to get to the top of, but just as it was in my grasp, I found myself slipping away. Over the next eighteen months I fell so hard and so far from that summit that I found myself at the bottom of a seabed, not knowing if I'd ever be able to rise again.

After Mumbai I was a media darling once more. In the press it was Monty Mania 2.0. Broadsheet journalists were writing articles about my second coming, with some saying (prematurely) that I was the man who'd ended Sachin Tendulkar's career.

My contribution to our seven-wicket win in the third Test in Calcutta was strong: 4-90 in the first innings and 1-75 in the second. The fourth Test in Nagpur was forgettable, but the draw won us the series. Andy Flower admitted it had been a mistake to leave me out for the first Test and my recall had helped turn the series around.

I think the depression started to take hold around the middle of 2012. Around this time my relationship with Dave Parsooth broke down as well, and I'd lost another voice that might have kept me on an even keel. Thanks to Neil Burns' methods and my success in India, I'd staved it off during the winter but back in Hove the voices were coming back, and with no cricket to focus on there was nothing to shut them up.

'You're no fucking good.'

'Fuck off!'

'You're no fucking good!'

'What the fuck would you know about it?'

'I know a shit batsman when I see one.'

And so on …

By now I knew there was a chance I was depressed, but I was hoping it wasn't as serious as it had been with Marcus. I clung to the fact that I still desperately wanted to play cricket and that as Marcus had been physically unable to get on a plane when his illness worsened, I couldn't be that bad if I still wanted to go to New Zealand.

For the first time, I went to get help and was prescribed anti-depressants. My head was almost permanently spinning and I was hearing all this white noise, but when I took them everything calmed down. It was great, but the side effects were worrying. The drugs increased my appetite. I'd always been around 85–86 kilos, but I was eating so I much I ballooned up to around 95–96 kilos, and it shows if you look at the footage of me on that tour of New Zealand.

This had to be the tour when Swanny got injured. I had my role as England's number one spinner back, but I was carrying 10 kilos of excess weight and my reactions were being dulled by the drugs. People assumed I'd 'let myself go' and KP claimed in his book that I'd been bullied by Matt Prior.

I can see why he thought that but it wasn't true. We were curt with each other on the field, because we wanted to win. Sometimes that might have come across as aggression and the body language (not to mention the actual language) might not have been great when someone let their standards slip in the field, but I was as guilty of that as anyone else, and significantly more so if you listen to my colleagues at Sussex.

I actually met up with Matt Prior and Stuart Broad quite recently when Matt was launching one of his sports nutrition products, and it was great. I went away thinking, why weren't we like that when we played together! And in fact we'd always got on OK; it's just that when we had our cricket heads on we were so focused on winning that it came at the expense of almost everything else.

***

I took 5-350 over the three drawn Test matches. The series ended on a modest high at Auckland when I survived five balls in a last wicket stand with Matt Prior, but as a bowler, I'd slipped back from the heights I'd reached in India.

This was Marcus's dilemma. He knew that if the medication was compromising his performance by even 2 or 3 per cent, it was enough to turn him from a world-class performer into someone more ordinary. On the other hand, if he didn't take the drugs, he might not be able to play at all.

In New Zealand, while using the medication, I was over 10 per cent heavier than usual and I was bowling at perhaps 70 per cent of my capacity. That wasn't enough against New Zealand, and it wasn't going to be enough against the Australians.

There was another option: I could have come clean as a player who suffered from mental health issues. This would have stopped people from saying I'd let myself go, but how many people recovered from 'outing' themselves as mentally ill and went on to have durable careers as international sportsmen?

Now I had to make the choice. With an Ashes summer ahead, I came off the drugs and entered a tailspin.

***

With my form and reputation once again tanking, my chances of playing against Australia now hinged on Swanny getting injured again. I also wasn't anywhere nearer the one-day squad and I was finding this increasingly hard to take. I knew, understood and accepted the reasons but I was now thirty-one years of age and could sense my career was slipping away from me.

My solution was to reinvent myself as a lower order batsman. If the selectors didn't want one-dimensional cricketers, I needed to add another dimension to my game.

I went back to Hove determined to improve my batting but ended up having a blazing row with Mark Robinson. I rigged up the bowling machine and started trying all these shots on the up. I was just whacking it everywhere (and really enjoying myself) when Robbo came in, looked at me and yelled: 'Monty, that is rubbish training! You cannot be training that way, you're a tailender and you've got to train like a tailender.'

His ideas were simple: if the ball was missing off stump, I leave it; if it's hitting off stump, I play it.

A year beforehand I'd have agreed with every word he said, but I started arguing with him. 'What if we need quick runs, Robbo?' Even as I was saying it I knew he was right and I was wrong, but I was putting huge pressure on myself and didn't want to back down. I was trying to do what Duncan Fletcher and Peter Moores had always wanted me to do, but I just didn't have the ability. At club cricket level I could have played these shots and made some useful runs, but at county level, more often than not they'd get me out. I wanted to cut like Robin Smith, cover drive like Michael Vaughan and switch hit like KP, but wanting to be able to do something and having the technique to actually do it are two very different things.

I felt like I was running uphill, into the wind, but I kept saying, 'No, I'm strong enough, keep going.'

I knew I was annoying Robbo and I knew I was alienating my teammates, over trivial things. For example, my shoulder was injured so when I was in the field I'd stop the ball with my boot and fling it back underarm. I thought

I was managing the injury. They thought I was taking the piss and a lot of reporters seemed to agree with them.

***

Yards thought I was introverted. I thought he was introverted. Robbo thought we were all introverted and that's why he'd brought in Lou Vincent for the 2011 season.

On the very same day Sussex announced Lou was joining us, we also signed Naved Arif from Pakistan, a left-arm seamer who qualified as a Kolpak player because his wife was Danish. As signings go this was like hiring Ronnie Biggs as head of security and employing Harold Shipman as your chief medical officer, not that we realised it at the time.

Lou had straggly, mullet-like hair, a wicked grin and an absolutely monstrous capacity for batting when he was in the mood. The problem was that whether Lou was 'in the mood' or not was frequently determined by extenuating circumstances.

He was known on the circuit as an eccentric, someone who'd drive his mobile home, the 'Worm Wagon', to matches, park in a field somewhere and catch his own breakfast in a nearby river. When I first met him I found him a really friendly guy and although he'd had mental health issues, he seemed to be in a good place. I can remember sitting in a car with him while he was explaining how moving his furniture around helped with his mindset, which wasn't something I'd ever heard of before.

He was doing a series of features for Sky Sports' *Cricket AM* show and he said he was absolutely loving it, but as Yards pointed out, he was one of the most extreme characters you could meet, veering between infectious enthusiasm and glowering depression.

Naved had a lower profile, but I'd shared a Cardiff-like last wicket stand with him during our Division One game with Lancashire at Hove earlier that summer. He made an unbeaten 100 and I batted out sixty-six balls for 17 to force a draw. When he wanted to he could bowl an unplayable delivery, but that was the problem. When, exactly, did he want to?

I'd really wanted to play in a one-day final at Lord's or a T20 finals day for Sussex, and in August 2011, we got to the quarter-finals of the T20 Cup. If we could beat Lancashire at Hove, I'd achieve one of those ambitions.

I bowled what cricinfo said was a 'superb spell', limiting them to 15 runs from four overs, during which they didn't score a single boundary and I'd tempted Karl Brown into a slog that was caught at long leg.

We restricted them to 152-8, which was gettable, but Lou was caught behind for a golden duck off the second ball of the innings, and we lost by 20 runs. That can happen and I didn't think a lot more of it at the time, but a few days later, we had a forty-over match against Kent and he was at it again.

This time he roped in Naved Arif to help. Naved went for 6.83 an over and took twenty-nine balls to score 11 runs, but again that can happen. Naved actually took a catch off my bowling, when we got Martin van Jaarsveld for 31, so he wasn't being obvious about it.

Even the best players have dips in form, which is why it's so difficult to detect. As an example, van Jaarsveld was a great fielder, but he managed to drop both Ed Joyce and Chris Nash from successive balls by Darren Stevens in the same match.

We put on 76 for the first wicket, but that brought Lou to the crease. He scored a single from his first six balls and then van Jaarsveld ran him out.

I saw it and thought, 'Oh mate ....', but that was all. It was poor cricket, but there had been plenty of that already as by that stage of the season both sides were basically dead on their feet. When he got to the dressing room, Yards said that in hindsight, Lou looked a bit too frantic asking everyone if they thought there was a run there. He thought it was a stage-managed show of anger. He was right: $14 million was bet on that match, in the Far East and India, and we all went away wondering how we could have blown it. If it had been 11 v 11, we'd probably have won, but it was 9 v 13, and even then we only lost by 14 runs.

All of this only emerged three years later, in 2014, when they were both banned for life. The last I heard of Lou he was trying reinvent himself as a landlord back in New Zealand, and there's no trace of Naved.

Kurt Cobain once said, 'Just because you're paranoid, don't mean they aren't after you.'

I was paranoid. But Lou and Naved really were trying to fuck us over.

***

By 2013, my paranoia was deepening and my behaviour was starting to worry my parents, so my mum arranged for me to meet a family friend she thought might be able to help me. I confided in him that I didn't feel great, that I was worried about the way everything was going and that I just didn't feel ... mentally correct.

He referred me to a Harley Street psychiatrist and I booked an appointment, but before our first session matters came to a head at a team barbecue in Hove in August.

Everything came out about how I felt and it probably came out the wrong way. I told Robbo I thought he'd let me down and said, 'I don't think you guys are really with me,' to my teammates. It wasn't true.

I was blaming everyone but myself while trying harder and harder to fight the depression.

In a way it was cathartic because my teammates realised I was suffering, but this had unintentionally devastating consequences for my career.

The night after the barbecue I was about to go to bed when Chris Nash sent me a text message saying, 'Come out for a beer.'

It was a Sunday night and I didn't want to go out, but I could see Chris was trying to include me. It was a sympathetic, human gesture and I thought if they're making an effort then I can make one too.

At this point a casual reader might be wondering about the cultural sensitivity of asking a Sikh to come out for a beer. Alastair Cook was rightly praised when he made sure Moeen Ali, a Muslim, wasn't drenched in champagne after England won the Ashes in 2015.

Sikhs aren't supposed to drink alcohol either, but in reality, a lot of us do.

I can vividly remember when I had my first drink. I was with my cousin. He gave me a bottle of Smirnoff Ice and said, 'Try this.' He said it was just a 'better form of lemonade'. And everyone used to love Smirnoff Ice, so I had it a couple of times and thought, 'Oh God, what's this feeling?'

I felt really happy and crazy, and they were like, 'Yeah man, this is alcohol!'

At university I drank a little bit, but not much. I mainly drank with my cousin, and then I started drinking with my mates at Luton Town & Indians who were at university as well, and I started to open up with them.

They thought I'd never drunk before, but I said, 'No, I've started drinking. It's quite cool!' They were initially shocked, but once that had subsided they said, 'Come and drink with us.' I started to make a lot more mates because I had something in common with them and it didn't give me any religious guilt feelings because my friends and my cousins were doing it too.

What I never quite got the hang of was drinking in any great volume. I think if I'd tried to keep pace with Wayne Larkins on a flight to Australia, or attended one of Beefy's barbecues, I might well have ended up dead!

As cricketers we'd drink every now and again when the schedule allowed, but in the post-Larkins era no one could drink pre-Larkins quantities of alcohol. Although there were times when Freddie gave it a reasonable go.

I hadn't built up that level of tolerance. It was a Sunday night in early August, in the middle of the Pride Festival. It was also in the middle of an Ashes series and if Swanny had picked up an injury, I would have been called into the squad. You can call it unprofessional, but I was bonding with my teammates, and 'mates' was the operative word: we were friends again, enjoying each other's company and getting steadily drunk, to the point where I really didn't know what I was doing any more.

We went to a vodka bar. Bad idea: vodka slips down too easily and when it's mixed with orange juice you don't even know you're drinking it. I don't remember how much I had, but from there we moved on to a night club called Shooshh, built into the arches on the seafront.

Here, I'm told, I was asked to leave.

By now I was out of it, to the extent I thought it would be a good idea to walk up a nearby ramp to the upper level of the promenade. The bouncer who'd thrown me out was standing right beneath the balcony and as I was absolutely hammered, I thought I'd get some revenge by tinkling over the edge.

Another bad idea. Maybe the worst I'd ever had.

He might have thought it was a drop of rain or something unsavoury from a bird ... until someone alerted him to me on the promenade. That was when they came after me. I don't blame them. I was an idiot. There's no defence for what I did and my only explanation is that I was drunk beyond reason.

I made a run for it. If I'd been thinking straight I would have headed inland and dived into a back street, or run onto the beach where it was dark. Then again, if I'd been thinking straight I wouldn't have fucking done it in the first place.

There are a thousand places someone can hide in a city like Brighton, but I decided to take refuge in a takeaway along the seafront.

Yet another bad idea. The selectors might have forgotten me, but the public haven't. I'm a drunk Sikh who plays cricket for England, so it's difficult to remain incognito in a brightly lit pizza parlour at four o'clock in the morning. It's also 2013, and everyone has a camera phone.

The bouncer has called for reinforcements. About a dozen of them have tracked me down. I get wrestled out of the building. My teammates arrive. I don't know how they find me or when they got here, but Rory Hamilton Brown looks like he's ready to go to war for me. Rory is prepared to fight a dozen bouncers, for me. He screams that he'll take them all on. He's doing this for me. My teammates are defending me when I've done something indefensible.

It's the ultimate team-building exercise. Or at least it would have been if the club weren't about to sack me.

I'm given a fixed penalty of £80, which might seem like a slap on the wrist, but the incident effectively kills my Sussex career.

I go back to my flat, sleep it off and wake up with my head aching, my organs failing, and in the middle of a hurricane of shit.

The camera phone footage goes viral. I go viral.

Sussex put out a statement saying they are launching a full investigation. After concluding this investigation, they sack me, although it isn't worded like that. A statement is put out in which I say: 'I am grateful to Sussex for allowing me to be released from my contract for 2014 and 2015 in order to explore other opportunities to further develop my cricket.'

Grateful to be released. Translation: they've sacked me and I'm being forced to thank them for it.

'I want to give myself the best chance of playing all forms of the game at the highest level. I have endured a challenging time this year off the field and my frustrations have sometimes got the better of me professionally. I apologise for letting the club, my colleagues and my fans down.' Translation: This is the excuse Sussex need to get rid of me and appease the retired colonels in the membership. Of whom there are many.

A story on the MailOnline attracted 366 comments. Some of these were transparently racist and they appeared unedited. Even at the time of writing this book, five years after the incident happened, these comments remain live on the *Mail's* site.

> *This man is not !!! English, we do not wear headgear !!*
>
> *English??????????*
>
> *Who would think that an English cricketer could be so vile ...*
>
> *He isn't English.*
>
> *A SLOB who should NEVER have played for England as he is NOT ENGLISH ... FACT.*

My Englishness was being denied by online commenters who were themselves struggling with their native language. And the idea that an Englishman might ever wear something on his head ...

There's no way a newspaper would publish something like this, but the internet is the Wild West.

The actual content of that story was largely accurate, but some of the other reporting was way off. 'Sources' told reporters that my family were ashamed of the humiliation I'd rained on them.

I'll be honest, they weren't pleased, but what they were telling me was this: it was a night out that went wrong. Keep it in perspective.

That, however, was the problem. By this stage in my life I was struggling to keep anything in perspective. My reality was becoming distorted by my condition. This incident accelerated my descent into full-blown mental illness.

Chapter 30

The Only Way is Essex

My timing was spectacular. At the precise moment I entered cricketing purdah, England, for the first time since 2009, decided they needed two spinners for a home Test, the final game of the series at The Oval.

I now realise I should have rung Mushtaq Ahmed. He was in Pakistan, but I should have contacted him and said, 'Look man, this is what's happened. I don't know what to do and I really need your help.'

I don't know why I didn't immediately because he was always there behind the scenes, checking up on me and asking if I was OK, but eventually I did get to see him at Lord's. He was coaching and I can remember helping him and giving the Kent bowler Imran Qayyum a few tips. When the session had finished we had some tea and he said, 'Look, man, you just need to bowl well in the next few games, take wickets and you'll be on the tour to Australia. If you do these thing right it helps me to go and say to the other guys, look he's behaving well, bowling well, he may not be taking wickets but you know what he can do.'

I think by then the EBC were coming round to the idea that, OK, he went out, had a few drinks and it went wrong, but he's gone to Essex and hopefully he'll be alright.

Forgive and forget, right? And a couple of things happened at The Oval that made forgiving and forgetting a lot more politically expedient.

The first was the performance of my replacement, Lancashire's Simon Kerrigan, the next cab off the rank. He'd done OK in the county championship, but he just wasn't ready for Test cricket. He was twenty-four so he was actually older than I'd been when I made my debut in India, but he hadn't played anything like as much first class cricket and he was still learning the craft. Shane Watson had monstered him in a tour match against the Lions and he only bowled eight excruciating overs in what proved to be his only Test.

People were speculating that he had the yips, a mental condition that can affect your motor functions, which was normally associated with golfers. Mike Selvey suggested it was maybe just stage fright, but it was painful to watch. He bowled full tosses and long hops, and Watson, once again, smashed him around The Oval.

By then, in a move that offered some symmetry to the start of my career, I'd rejected an offer to join Northants and had instead signed on loan with Essex. The Northants boys thought I was going to be playing with them right up until the morning of the county championship match against Essex at Colchester, but Neil Burns recommended me to Paul Grayson, who thought I might be able to spin them to promotion and decided I was worth a gamble.

A posse of reporters turned up to Castle Park looking for a scoop, but Sussex had explicitly instructed me not to talk to anyone and with my career on the line, I had to comply. To be honest, it was nice to have an excuse not to talk. I was never really a natural in press conferences. Reporters used to roll their eyes when they heard I'd been put up for the interviews and they'd count the number of times I used the word 'areas'.

I took a couple of wickets, but it was a batsman's track and the game ended in a draw after the third day was wiped out by rain.

It wasn't the sort of performance the selectors would have taken a lot of notice of, but for the fact that while I was toiling on a dead wicket at an outground 60 miles from London, Simon Kerrigan's international career was coming to an end at The Oval.

I had to feel sorry for him, even though I knew his performance meant I was almost certain to get a place on the Ashes tour.

The other potential barrier to my selection was removed after the match had ended in a draw and my erstwhile England teammates started using the outfield at The Oval as a makeshift urinal. Having won the series 3-0, they were celebrating by drinking a few beers out on the pitch. They assumed that everyone had gone home and as they couldn't be arsed to walk to the toilets back in the dressing room, they just unzipped and unleashed, right out in the middle.

It was dark, but in the press box one of the Australian hacks was killing time when he spotted something that looked a bit like a group of grown men having a synchronised piss on a cricket square.

It was Urinegate 2.0. Pick up a newspaper the following day and you'd have thought English cricket was drowning in piss. 'What is it with England's cricketers and urine?' ran one headline, and you can probably write most of the others yourself. Social commentators queued up to disown us. Politicians were disowning us. The Australian media pretended to be outraged when in reality they were borderline ecstatic that they had a reason to look down on us after getting their biggest hiding in decades.

One of the unexpected consequences was that it was now going to be difficult for the ECB to exclude me from an Ashes tour for any ethical reasons. The moral high ground had gone, even though I wouldn't claim any equivalence between what I did when I was off my face on a balcony and what they did on a patch of grass when they thought no one was watching.

I stayed with Essex and kept my head down. We didn't get promoted, but I took a few wickets, got a deal for the 2014 season and got myself on the tour.

That was like being handed a first class seat for the *Titanic*. Minus the thousand miles of pleasurable, trouble-free sailing before we hit the iceberg.

Chapter 31

Getting Beaten up for Ten Rounds

This 2013 version of the *Titanic* set sail from Stoke. That probably should have told us something.

It was autumn 2013 and I, Monty Panesar, was struggling.

The ECB, however, remained unaware of my condition and they wanted me to attend a pre-Ashes team-building weekend, in which we performed immersive role-playing exercises, pretending to be spies. As ideas go, this was a bit like sending an alcoholic to an all-inclusive resort with Ian Botham and Phil Tufnell.

This might have been a good moment to flag up my condition, but given that I was still in the doghouse, I was reluctant to do anything that might lessen the idea I was a 'team player'.

We spent hours in a fucking classroom in darkest Staffordshire being briefed on how to use two-way radios as well as on the phonetic alphabet we were supposed to use on them.

'What the Foxtrot Uniform Charlie Kilo are we doing here, over?'

'I don't know, but I think they're making us look like a right bunch of Charlie Uniform November Tangos, over.'

Our mission, which we had to choose to accept, was to follow a pair of 'terrorists' around the Potteries, watch them when necessary and report on their movements, all while blending in with the environment.

No, me neither. You try finding a tree in Burslem that looks like a 6' 1" man with a beard and a patka.

Boyd Rankin was supposedly on surveillance. At 6' 8" tall, he was crammed into a car for hours. Incredibly he suffered cramps and wasn't fully fit for the series. Swanny spent fifteen hours in a Morrisons car park. I'm amazed he didn't have mental health issues by the time that ordeal was over. Trotty was supposed to be watching one of the terrorists outside a pub, but at the exact moment his quarry made his escape, he was too busy signing an autograph to notice he'd gone.

Stuart Broad and Ben Stokes were parked up outside a building at 5 am when they saw a light come on and a bloke light up a huge joint. He shat himself because he thought they were the police.

This was days before we were due to fly out. It was a complete waste of time and by the time it was over we'd all reached the conclusion the management had to be taking the Papa India Sierra Sierra.

***

They called it the 'Pomnishambles'. We should have hired Wayne Larkins as our entertainment manager for that Ashes tour. Fuck it, we should have made him director of cricket; the end result wouldn't have been any worse and at least we might have had a few laughs.

Wayne would have got the beers in, KP, Matt Prior and Swanny could have had a card school going at the back of the plane and we could have got Andy Flower on the karaoke machine, singing a bit of Abba in between swigs from his thirty-sixth can of the flight.

I might not be a doctor in the field of mental health but if anyone wants my input for a case study, I can give them a few pointers:

- Don't go on a cricket tour where members of your team have been running a spoof Twitter account laughing at your star player.

- Avoid facing late-blossoming fast bowlers who've been waiting four years to extract a humiliating revenge on you because your fans suggested their 'bowling was shite'.

- Try to steer clear of stressful environments, such as dressing rooms where batsmen are crying.

- Never assume that the player being selected ahead of you won't decide to retire with immediate effect three games into a series.

- Don't make the mistake of preparing for said tour with a training camp where you forget you're cricketers and start to believe you're in MI5.

***

Somehow it was the bowlers' fault. I didn't play in the first Test at the Gabba and hadn't expected to, but in the nightmare of bitterness and recrimination that followed, people forgot that at the end of day one, Stuart Broad had waltzed into the press conference, clutching all the newspapers that had fired him up that morning, with 6-81.

They were all out for 295, which looked pretty meagre until Mitchell Johnson turned into someone who bowled like the lovechild of Curtly Ambrose and Waqar Younis.

The word had gone round the dressing room that he'd been bowling 'rockets' during the ODI series back in England, but his first six overs went for 32 and he was bowling, as the song went, to the left and to the right.

Then he clicked. He was already in Trotty's head from the moment he hit him on the helmet in a one-dayer back in England. Trotty had suffered a breakdown as a result and from then on, it's easy to say, he should never have gone on the tour. I was hiding my condition. He couldn't; and when you see a player like Trotty – England's rock – break down and cry, you can imagine the effect that has on a team.

KP later said when he saw Johnson bowling he thought he might die, out there on the Gabbatoir. A year later, Phil Hughes did die after being hit on the head by a bouncer, but it was a tragic, one-in-a-billion event. If you really thought you'd die, you wouldn't play the game – you couldn't.

KP thought the fear was tangible in the dressing room.

We hadn't prepared for Johnson, and even after Brisbane we still felt he might just have got lucky. That this was his Devon Malcolm 9-57 innings when everything he tried came off. Or at least some of us did.

The other batsmen thought their plans were OK; they just hadn't executed them properly. Johnson had exploited the world's quickest pitch and fair play to him, but he wouldn't be so lucky on an English-style Bunsen at Adelaide.

Au contraire.

***

I was back in the team for the second Test. When I bowled Steve Smith for 6 in their first innings they were 174-4 and vulnerable, but that brought Brad Haddin in and he was their unsung hero of that series. We regularly got them five down relatively early and he bailed them out every time. Haddin was brilliant. I bowled forty-four overs in that innings and took 1-157.

Swanny bowled thirty-six overs, even though he could hardly feel his hand any more. He said it was pure luck he took two wickets.

Johnson, meanwhile, took 6-16 in the space of twenty-six balls, but I stuck it out for thirty-six deliveries before he bowled me. That was one thing you could say for my batting: I was never frightened of fast bowlers.

I got Michael Clarke in their second innings, but they were just batting to set us a target at the point. Our second innings was more respectable but we still lost by 218 runs and the 'clear the air' meeting afterwards went about as well as clear the air meetings usually go. It filled the air with poison.

We learned that the defeat was apparently the bowlers' fault. As it was obvious that Johnson was blowing the top order away, we should have dug in, instead of playing shots. I was sitting there thinking, 'Hang on, I just batted out more deliveries than Cookie, KP, Ben Stokes and Matt Prior combined.'

KP sat there, whistling silently and looking out of the window, but Graham Gooch went for Swanny and Broad, telling them they hadn't scored enough runs. 'We're eight and nine for a reason, Graham,' Stuart replied, adding that it was one thing chipping in another 100 runs when the team already had 300 on the board, as they regularly did; it was quite another when you're running into Mitchell Johnson after he'd only bowled three overs.

It was like a beautifully spoken public schoolboy talking back to his Essex Man headmaster.

It didn't matter that he had a point. Graham just lost it: 'Don't blame our batsmen; it's your fault, you've got to chip in daaahn the aw-dah!'

Broady had actually been our second top scorer at the Gabba, quite aside from the fact he'd taken 6-81 there. If we'd had a few more like him we might not have been in this position, but the top order and the coaching staff were in denial.

They, England's elite batsmen, didn't know how to play Johnson, but it was still our fault. Maybe we should have picked eleven bowlers?

At this point, that car park in Stoke was looking like a decent option.

***

I was dropped for the third Test, even though Swanny had, by now, lost most of the feeling in his bowling arm. He didn't want to play, but Cookie told him he needed his senior players. They brought Tim Bresnan in to shore up the lower order, and despite my heroic thirty-five-ball 2 in Adelaide, I was out again.

We lost by a mere 150 runs this time and Swanny retired with immediate effect. I honestly didn't think he'd been bowling that badly, but his arm was a lot worse than we realised and he was effectively playing from memory.

Even so, it was still a shock that he'd given up completely, but I think with Graeme Swann, cricket wasn't a matter of life or death. Some people have got the kind of intensity where they can't let go of it, but Swanny had a great option of going into *Test Match Special*. If he didn't have that option, do you reckon he would have retired? Absolutely not, but he knew he had a job lined up and that's why he took that exit route strategy. Would you retire if you didn't have another job in place? He got hammered for it, but I thought it was a good move from him. He'd achieved everything he needed to.

In the court of public opinion he was crucified. All the usual suspects were having a go, but even people like Freddie and Michael Vaughan were piling in.

Ex-pros were calling him a 'tosser' and worse in private for not seeing out the tour, but he felt he was hindering the team.

I could understand why, because I was in a similar situation. I was probably playing when I wasn't fit to.

If you're on a tour you're always ready to come in, but the truth is, I wasn't at my maximum. Losing every game felt like being in a ring and getting beaten senseless for ten rounds.

It was summed up by the fourth Test in Melbourne. We got a 51-run first innings lead but still only set them a target of 231.

I had Chris Rogers caught by Johnny Bairstow during the chase, but by then he'd already made 116. At 2.30 pm, I ran in to bowl to Shane Watson. He played it through square leg, they ran two runs and clinched an eight-wicket victory.

I haven't bowled for England since, although if Joe Root is reading this – Joe, I am still available.

***

There was a point during that tour when I thought, 'Cricket's not for me.' I'd had enough of it. It passed fairly quickly but it was that kind of tour.

When Michael Clarke told Jimmy Anderson to 'get ready for a broken fucking arm', it indicated a level of obnoxiousness we hadn't previously seen in the Australian side, one that was rising even higher by the time Moeen Ali was called 'Osama' a couple of summers later. It wasn't a sledge; it was a threat.

In hindsight you could detect the seeds of the great Australian ball-tampering scandal.

When I did my MBA in International Sports Management I learned a lot about team dynamics. I studied Guardiola and Wenger, and in any team sport you're always going to have some big players. It's how the great players handle themselves that defines a team's integrity. If you're one of the top ten players in the world, you have huge influence in the dressing room and beyond.

It's political power, and a great player has to ask himself how he'll use that. Will he or she help his or her teammates, give them opportunities and encourage them to improve? Or will they abuse their power?

I think that's what happened in that team. The ball-tampering incident was caused by a couple of very strong characters, who would then force the youngsters to behave in the way they did. When you get to that level you have a choice. Do you say we're going to win at all costs, or do you win in the right way?

Chapter 32

Paranoia

There is no such thing as paranoia. Your worst fears can come true at any moment.

Hunter S. Thompson

My England career ended at the MCG.

My Essex career effectively ended in the Virgin Active Gym, Chelmsford, a grey building bolted onto a housing estate, next to the headquarters of Essex County Cricket Club.

The record shows I took forty-two wickets for Essex in the 2014 county championship season. I'm not entirely sure how.

The tone for the season was set by an incident in the gym, when I had another public meltdown in front of someone I really couldn't afford to offend. I'd known the captain, James Foster, for years and he'd been really keen for me to sign for Essex the previous season. As his voice carried weight with the decision makers I was in his debt, but one stupid incident in the gym ruined my reputation with him and the rest of the squad.

The shit hit the extractor when we were on the exercise bikes and it started to get competitive. It was the sort of thing that happens every day in every gym in the world: two guys trying to outdo each other. A bit of macho posturing, a bit of showing off, but nothing serious.

I was off the meds, however, and although I was physically fitter than I had been in Australia, my inner Don Logan started talking again.

'Fossy's trying to show you up.'

'No he isn't.'

'Yes he is. Look, he thinks he's Bradley Wiggins. He's trying to make you look a right c**t.'

'Fuck off, no he isn't!'

'Look! All the Academy boys are here! He's trying to look good in front of them and mug you off in the process!'

Don wouldn't shut up. If Fossy was Bradley Wiggins I was going to be Chris Froome. We nearly broke the fucking bikes. The Academy boys were egging us on because they just thought we were racing, and then I snapped.

'You fuckers are all against me! Fuck the fucking lot of you!'

I stormed out in a rage and as soon as I felt the fresh air outside I knew I'd fucked up. What do I do? Go back and apologise? Too humiliating. If I'd been thinking straight I'd have realised it would have limited the damage, but again, if I'd been thinking straight I wouldn't have done it in the first place.

Paul Grayson eventually found me and asked what was going on. I said, 'Look, I got a bit angry, but I was competing with Fossy and I just lashed out when I should have kept my mouth shut.'

He was quite understanding. He just said take two weeks off and don't go to that gym during that time, presumably because he was hoping it would blow over.

It might have done if I hadn't shot myself in the foot with my timekeeping again. I came back, bowled well in the tour match against Sri Lanka, was easing my way back in and then, on the morning of our county championship game with Glamorgan, I lost track of the time.

I was still in my flat at 10.30 when I realised the match was due to start at 11.

'Ooooooooooooohhhhh fuuuuccccccckkkkk!'

I felt physically sick. It was like a flashback to the time I'd turned up late and I thought Kepler Wessels was going to punch me, a horrible feeling when I knew I was in the wrong and all I could do was get to the dressing room as quickly as possible and hope the sentence wouldn't be too severe.

Unlike Kepler, I didn't think Fossy would punch me, but his punishment was worse: 'Sorry Monty, I'm dropping you for timekeeping.'

I apologised. I said I was sorry and I meant it, but it was futile. They were playing without me. I wasn't a kid any more; I was a 32-year-old senior professional who was supposed to be setting an example to the younger players. I was still in the doghouse for the gym meltdown and I knew I didn't have a leg to stand on, but the way they handled it just made me angrier.

I'd seen plenty of cover stories used in cricket for players who'd turned up drunk and thought they were bowling at nine stumps. Paul Smith of Warwickshire once went out to face Malcolm Marshall when he was, in his own words, 'three sheets to the wind'.

Marshall took one look at him, said, 'Don't worry, Smitty boy, this won't take long,' and got him out within minutes. Cricketing euthanasia and no one knew a thing about it until Smith brought his book out a few years later.

My shoulder injury could have flared up. My ankle might have been sore. It didn't need to be a big deal but Essex put out a statement saying I'd been dropped for timekeeping. What a time for the media department of a cricket club to finally discover the virtue of honesty.

Of course it's possible they'd had enough of covering for me and were trying to shame me into changing my behaviour, but it didn't work. I continued to do things I cannot attempt to defend, only explain. I ignored team warm-ups and warmed up on my own. When asked to bowl I would refuse if I didn't get the field setting I wanted.

Graham Gooch once said the only way he could get Devon Malcolm to do anything was to instruct him to do the exact opposite. I was probably worse. If I disagreed with the team strategy, I would refuse to bowl. There is no excuse for this, only an explanation: I was mentally ill. I was putting so much pressure on myself that I couldn't accept reality any more.

I only understood what I'd put Paul Grayson and James Foster through a couple of years later when I did my Level 3 coaching and I saw one kid who was acting like he was hard and different to all the others. I looked at him and thought of Duncan, Robbo, Andy Flower and Paul Grayson. If they could have seen me at that moment they might have smiled.

***

After the Glamorgan incident, Monty Mania became a distant memory. On cricinfo, David Hopps wrote:

> One of the most beloved England cricketers of his age, at 32, is losing his appeal. He has recently been photographed on the field wearing spectacles – and very earnest they make him look, too – but it is himself he needs to look at. Cricket, it seems, no longer puts a smile on his face. A general disenchantment seems to run deep.

He didn't know the half of it. In 2015 I played a couple of county championship games for Essex before it was announced I was taking an 'indefinite break'.

I wasn't quite done. In early August I was back in the Essex first team for the festival match at Colchester against Surrey and I took 4-112 in their first innings, including some notable scalps. Steve Davies shouldered arms to one that spun more than he expected and crashed into his off-stump, and I also duped Jason Roy into a stumping.

Unfortunately my fielding was almost self-parodying. At one point the ball went through my legs to the long off boundary and I could hear a derisive cry of 'fielded Monty' from a heckler who was merely saying what my teammates were almost certainly thinking.

I made up for it with some more athletic stops on the boundary towards the end of the innings, but it just illustrated Graham Dilley's law: You'll always get remembered for the one bad over you've had in the field.

At the end of the season they released me. I don't blame them. If the umpires turned down an appeal, I'd get angry with them. If my teammates dropped a chance, I'd get angry with them. If I went for runs, I'd get angry in general. KP once said: 'It's tough being me in the dressing room.' By the end of 2014, it was tough being me in any dressing room, but it was even tougher for the people around me.

Chapter 33

Help

I was Monty Panesar the geo-political symbol, the man who embodied the integration of two of the world's great nations, England and India, yet I couldn't even integrate with my own teammates.

I was Monty Panesar the brand, but I couldn't sell myself to my own employers.

I became the dark secret of the county circuit, a self-fulfilling prophecy. Because of my paranoia, people were now talking behind my back but where mention of my name might once have raised a smile, now it raised eyebrows and caused knowing rolls of eyeballs.

I moved back into the family home outside Luton and pushed my parents, brother and sister to breaking point. We were watching a replay of one of my matches on television and they started teasing me about my fielding.

I snapped. It was nothing I hadn't heard a thousand times before, but I turned round and screamed at them: 'Why didn't you tell me this before? Why are you laughing now?'

The truth was, a bit of me had always hated people laughing at me for my fielding. In the past I'd shrugged it off, but in my condition I thought even my family were against me.

My behaviour became so bad around them and my anger with them so great that they told me they couldn't handle me any more. There was never a specific intervention, but at one point they said, 'Look, if this is how you're going to behave, at least get your own flat, because we can't deal with this. There's only so much support we can give you.'

They were ordering me to get help. I did, but the nature of my condition made getting help difficult. I felt like I was a ball of fire and that if anyone tried to pick me up I'd burn their hand. In my head I thought the cricket community was shunning me. I also thought the Sikh community wouldn't come near me because I was bringing shame on them.

On both counts I was proved wrong, but it took me a long time to realise it.

People in the game were trying to help me. Even without taking into account all my other disciplinary lapses, like timekeeping and showing dissent to umpires, for refusing to bowl during a match, Essex had grounds to dismiss me. Instead they honoured our two-year deal and paid me throughout. They also put me in touch with the PCA mental health ambassador, which helped set the wheels in motion for my recovery.

The cricket circuit isn't huge and while I got on with almost everyone and had never made enemies, I realised a lot of my teammates didn't really know me.

In 2013, I'd made an appearance on *Soccer AM* where they invited questions from various celebrities. One of them was from my then county and country teammate Matt Prior: 'What does he do in the evenings on tour? No one ever sees him.' True. I explained I was revising for an exam at the time.

James Anderson said, 'I don't have much on Mont.' Also true. At that point there wasn't much to have.

When I look back at that interview with Helen Chamberlain and Max Rushden, I'm confident and relaxed. They showed footage of me diving to make my ground during the final Test with New Zealand, and I said, 'My diving's a bit like Didier Drogba's.'

I was at ease and exchanging genuinely light-hearted banter about my batting in front of a live television audience well into the tens of thousands, if not significantly higher. On the basis of that clip I could have been a regular on the chat show circuit – and indeed, if Graham Norton or Jonathan Ross happen to be reading this, I am available. Call my agent Clive. Let's sort something out.

In short, I was precisely the last person you'd expect to be suffering from mental health issues. After Marcus, Freddie, Yards and Jonathan Trott.

I had good relationships with both Matt and Jimmy and our last-wicket stands against Australia and New Zealand are shared memories we'll have forever. But maybe if I'd gone out and got hammered with them we might have had a closer bond. It had to be a better way of getting to know someone than spending a night sitting in a car park in Stoke, and it might have increased my tolerance before that disastrous night in Brighton.

There are people now, like Geraint Jones and Andy Flower, whom I feel I can call at any time if I need help. In fact with Andy, if you ring him he makes you feel like he's honoured that you've asked him!

At the time, however, most of my real confidants were civilians.

At the highest level, team sport can cultivate paranoia.

In 2016, the Professional Footballers' Association revealed that 165 of its members had sought help for mental health issues, predominantly depression, stress, anxiety and anger. The main causes were insecurity. Players were living in an almost permanent state of anxiety about their performances, their contracts and their management.

Cricket isn't quite as volatile as football, where some teams change managers every six months and players move a lot more frequently, but all of the above applied in our sport, as did the perception that because we earn more than the average worker we should somehow be inoculated to the effects of mental illness.

If left unchecked, mental health issues can destroy lives.

They can also end them. I was never tempted to self-harm and I didn't have suicidal thoughts, but a horrifying number of cricketers have committed suicide. The Australian author David Frith once wrote a book about some of the men who'd taken their own lives, called *By His Own Hand*. The foreword for the first edition was written by the former Somerset captain Peter Roebuck, who subsequently committed suicide by jumping out of a sixth-floor window in a Cape Town hotel. Roebuck apparently threw himself to his death after having been told South African police wanted to question him regarding an alleged sexual assault, which had, in turn, reportedly left the alleged victim suicidal.

Prior to Roebuck's death, Frith had published an updated version of *By His Own Hand* under the title *Silence of the Heart*. The foreword for this version was provided by the former England captain Mike Brearley, who later practised as a psychoanalyst and had worked with a number of near-suicidal patients.

When analysing their motives he said they were often 'dominated by one part of their psyche only, by the side which is cut off from love and value and drives them towards death and negativity … they may have grandiose, unrealistic ideas about how brilliant they ought to be.'

Brearley openly wondered if he could have done more to help David Bairstow, who'd killed himself at the age of forty-six, when his son, the future England batsman and wicketkeeper Jonny, was just eight.

Although he concluded that there always were multiple and complex reason's for every cricketer's death and that the game alone could not be blamed in every case, as Frith pointed out, the suicide rates among cricketers were still significantly higher than they were for the wider population.

If I'd been born twenty years earlier, I don't know how this would have played out, but by 2014, cricket had a far better idea of how its players suffered. Thanks to Marcus and others after him, there were now structures in place.

These may well have saved my career, and Brearley himself would play an integral role in my recovery.

Chapter 34

Montage (Part 2)

In the Martin Scorsese-directed biopic of my life, this is where the second montage kicks in. A two-year period is condensed into two minutes, while a Rolling Stones track plays in the background.

We cut to a scene where I lay on a couch in Mike Brearley's office, as he strokes his chin and I wave my arms, before I suddenly have a eureka moment, stand up and embrace him. We cut to a scene where I run through the streets of Stopsley in grey jogging pants, and a sweatshirt, as crowds of schoolchildren shout 'Monty! Monty!' as I sprint past. We cut to a scene in an unidentifiable wilderness, where a wizened old man, played by Anthony Hopkins, watches as I perform yoga in a vest.

We cut back to the rain-sodden streets of Bury Park, where a local milkman (a cameo role for Benedict Cumberbatch, perhaps) waves at me from his float while I'm on a 5 am training run. We cut to the nets of Luton Town & Indians, where I rebuild my action under the gaze of John Emburey and Mushtaq Ahmed, played by Brian Cox and Morgan Freeman.

We cut to the steps of Luton Town Hall, where I sprint to the top before letting out a roar that can be heard across the whole of Bedfordshire. And as the music reaches a crescendo, we cut to me, walking through the Long Room at Lord's, high-fiving members in their bacon and custard ties as I make my England recall. In the final scene, these same members abandon the pavilion and invade the pitch as I take the wicket that clinches the Ashes and they hoist me on their shoulders. The final frame freezes with a picture of me grinning as I parade an urn the size of the European Champions League trophy in front of the pavilion. Then the credits roll.

***

The fantasy was nice, but my recovery was a slow and at times painful process. At one point I went to see a hypnotherapist called Peter Gilmour, who specialised in helping sportsmen and women.

He'd spent a while assessing me in an environment where I was comfortable, among non-cricketing friends in a café. I can remember the first five minutes of the conversation, but after that I was just rambling incoherently.

They told me I should go to see Peter, but after our first session I was shaking uncontrollably. He said he'd never had a session like it and thought he'd broken something in me. 'I think you're suffering from low self-confidence,' he said. That sounded about right, but I wasn't ready for the follow-up. 'I also think what you've got is paranoid schizophrenia.'

I was stunned. 'Are you kidding me?'

He wasn't. I thought back to the barbecue in Hove and the meltdown in the gym. I thought back to the way I'd reacted to my family when they'd joked about my fielding. Paranoia made sense, but schizophrenia?

The first thing you do, after the shock subsides, is Google the symptoms. According to Wikipedia, schizophrenia is ...

'mental disorder characterised by abnormal behaviour ...'

That sounded like me.

'A decreased ability to understand reality ...

That also sounded like me.

'Common symptoms include false beliefs ...'

Guilty.

'Unclear or confused thinking ...'

And again.

'Hearing voices that others do not, reduced social engagement and emotional expression, and a lack of motivation.'

I should have drawn up a bingo card.

***

One of Neil Burns' strengths is that he's a very caring guy and if he can't help you, he'll know someone who can. It was Neil's idea to put me in touch with Mike Atherton when I first revealed I had mental health issues and he wrote a brilliant article as a result.

It was also Neil who suggested I get in touch with Mike Brearley when he realised I needed specialist treatment.

Brearley agreed to see me and I met him at his practice in London.

I obviously knew of Brearley's reputation and he'd always had an aura about him. Part of his mystique was because he was maybe the only England captain of the past forty years who wasn't involved with the media in some capacity. He had a first class degree in Classics and a 2:1 in Moral Sciences from Cambridge, and he'd made a career as a psychoanalyst after retiring.

He'd quit at the top, at the end of the 1981 Ashes series, and since then his legend had grown precisely because he limited his public appearances. When he did say something, you knew it was worth listening to.

The first thing he said to me was that we had to keep our meeting between ourselves and that we couldn't tell anyone what was happening.

Although he subsequently said he was happy for me to reveal that he'd helped me in this book, I don't want to reveal too much of what we said during those private sessions. I can say that he identified things for me and broke things down. As an example he told me to be careful how I spoke to people, because the things you say can put thoughts in their mind that can make them feel a bit weird and random.

He recognised I was probably in a place where I wasn't connected with reality and said when you're confidence is low, that's when these random thoughts start coming into your mind. When your confidence is high, it's like your head is emerging from the water and you can see everything clearly, and when your confidence is low, it's like you're under the water.

***

Brearley also told me I had to manage what thoughts I was putting into my mind, and what ended up happening was I thought, 'Sod it, I'm not going to put thoughts into my mind, I'm going to listen to the holy book.'

I believe the biggest single factor in my recovery was reconnecting with my faith.

When I met Sikh cricket fans, they usually suggested I should go to the gurdwara and start praying again and in the end I stopped the pills and I went back to the Guru Grant Sahib, our holy text.

I'd put off going back to the temple in Coventry for a long time but when I finally returned, I felt this sense of peace. I felt connected to Sikhism again and I started to visit more and more. I remembered my visits there when I was a kid and I'd play instruments on the stage. I felt like some of my memory had been lost and now I was connecting to all the good things I used to do. It really helped me. It made me realise that I'd been to the bottom of the seabed. I was drowning but I floated back, and when my relationship with God is really healthy, then my relationships with other people are good.

It's like God is saying, 'If you keep me close to you, other people will like you and that energy of love that you have is through me.'

We all believe in the oneness, and Guru Nanak said you need to be a better human being first, then be a religious person. My way of doing that was going to the temple and connecting to my religion once again. The mind is like a jar: you fill it with positivity and suddenly there's no room for negative thoughts any more.

I spent some time in Australia, where they're less likely to use medication than in England. They use physical activity for fitness because it releases endorphins, which act as an anti-depressant. So I'd go for a run, go to the gym and I also did a lot of yoga. I'd go to the gym and come back really exhausted, but my reality was different when I came out to how it had been when I went in.

I was healing and I was ready to go back to the world of cricket. If they'd have me.

Chapter 35

'You're Monty Fucking Panesar!'

With my shoulder needing rehabilitation I needed to ease my way back into the game, so I accepted an offer of £500 per game to play for Totteridge Milhillians.

They weren't your average club side, but then Totteridge, a village enclave about 10 miles north of Central London, isn't your average place. Arsene Wenger lives there, although he's apparently in what passes for Totteridge's ghetto, while his ex-boss, David Dein, is nearby in a house that, legend has it, contains its own bat cave.

The club itself had a reputation for being the kind of place star players would hang out, without getting bothered by anyone who might feel like bothering them. It was the sort of place where you might get half a dozen spectators, yet Justin Langer and Darren Sammy had both played there in the past, and when I joined, Eoin Morgan used to roll the wicket. More importantly, my old Loughborough University mate Steve Selwood was Head of Operations there.

It was a great way of easing myself back into the cricketing network. My reputation, by then, travelled before me and there'd apparently been some scepticism about whether or not I'd turn up. Someone said, 'I'll believe it when he's at the end of his run-up,' but when I defied expectations and turned up for my first match I was surprised how genuinely pleased to see me everyone was.

My bowling partner was John Emburey, who, although he was sixty-three, could still land the ball on a spot and skittle the average village side.

John and I would sit in the clubhouse drinking tea and talking about bowling. At that point, aged thirty-three, I was still dreaming of becoming The Greatest Spin Bowler in the World once again, but being at Totteridge created other opportunities.

Steve mentioned a guy who came along for batting practice called Clive Hart, who was part of a company called Shooting Stars Management.

I'm not sure how high my self-esteem was at the time, because Monty Mania had bitten the dust and it hadn't yet occurred to me that I might end up on programmes with the word 'Master' in the title.

When I asked Clive why he thought I might be in demand, his exact words were: 'You're Monty fucking Panesar!' Clive says I 'looked right through' him when we'd started the conversation, but that got my attention, as did his subsequent rant, in which he said, 'Have you even watched a fucking reality show recently? You can get on TV if you've slept with Calum Best and the only reason he's fucking famous is because he's George Best's son! You've taken 167 wickets for England!'

***

I started playing for the PCA's England Masters side, and for Lashings, a legends team who toured the country playing club sides and raising money for a number of charitable organisations. This was where I first met Henry Blofeld. I hadn't really 'got' him until that point. You don't often get a chance to listen to *Test Match Special* if you're playing cricket and I'd always seen Henry as part of an elite, a member of cricket's inner circle. For a lot of the clubs we visited, Henry was a bigger draw than most of the players.

He'd turn up at matches looking like a flamboyant country squire, in a chequered cap and sunglasses, a bottle green jumper and a pair of trousers so bright they were probably visible from space.

I'd never been able to work out if he'd called me 'Monty Python' deliberately for a cheap laugh or if he'd just had a senior moment. As soon as I heard him commentate in the flesh, I realised it was the latter. He'd do a live commentary on the first innings, usually from a portable table next to the scorers.

Martin Bicknell was our captain, but he kept confusing him with his brother Darren.

(At this point I should make a confession: I called Leicester's then manager Craig Shakespeare 'William' during an interview with *Arsenal TV*, so I can see how it happens.)

The reason he called everyone 'my dear old thing' was because he hardly ever remembered their names.

The only time he definitely didn't get confused was when he was trying to sell you something. He had a boot load of Blowers merchandise at every match, with books, audio books, *TMS* mugs with caricatures and bottles of 'Blowers' Own' wine, one of which was a white burgundy, the other a red Cotes du Rhône. It was fifteen quid a bottle, and £2.50 extra if you wanted him to sign the label. No freebies, but he'd knock off a fiver if you ordered a case.

At one match, at Sutton Valence in Kent, Lashings were playing a House of Commons and Lord's Select XI, who, despite the name, were actually a team of Tory MPs no one had heard of, other than John Redwood. Blowers was chatting to a couple of them during the innings break in a voice that was slightly too loud to be considered discrete. 'Do you have much to do with the squeaker?' he said, his mouth curdling with distaste. He meant the speaker, John Bercow, and this wasn't one of his senior moments. The MPs looked a bit uncomfortable and said something vague, but Blowers assumed he was among friends and started letting rip. 'I really can't abide that man; he's just so vulgar …'

He went on for a while till a man in a green body warmer and wellingtons tapped him on the shoulder.

'You do realise that your microphone is on, don't you?'

With no Peter Baxter to cut him off, he'd been broadcasting to the entire ground. 'Don't worry, I agree with you,' the man in the wellingtons said, trying to reassure him. Sutton Valence was that kind of place.

***

I tried to make a comeback with Northants for the 2016 season. Injuries prevented me from showing what I could do but it was still a positive experience.

When I went back everyone was so welcoming and so nice that I remember sitting on a bench in the pavilion and thinking, 'What's going on?'

I used to think these fans and these people were against me and I realised it wasn't true at all. Something was different and I felt a really positive connection.

They wanted to sign me for a year but my shoulder wasn't strong enough, so I carried on playing for the PCA and Lashings and had a few games for Bedfordshire in 2017.

I made a few headlines at the start of the 2018 season when I wrote to the eighteen first-class counties asking for a trial, but by then I was still trying to recover from a broken ankle I'd sustained while training for *Dancing on Ice* (don't worry, I'll come to that in due course).

I didn't get any first class offers so I signed for Hornchurch in the Essex League, and despite my injuries, I took fifty-six wickets during the 2018 season.

With the plate out of my ankle and my body recovering, I'm not yet ready to retire. I'll be thirty-seven at the start of the 2019 season, but that's not that old for a spin bowler. John Emburey was forty when he played in the 1993 Ashes series and he was arguably the only batsman who'd figured out how to play Shane Warne. Maybe that's where Graham Gooch got his ideas about the bowlers digging in from?

I'm still hoping to make a first class comeback, but I'll carry on playing club cricket for as long as my body will let me.

And when I do finally have to give it up, there are other options …

Chapter 36

Can a Vegetarian Eat Blended Camel Foreskin?

Clive was right. I was 'Monty Fucking Panesar' and I was in demand for TV work. In autumn 2016 I went into advanced negotiations to appear on *I'm a Celebrity … Get Me Out of Here*.

I was in Australia anyway because I was playing grade cricket in Sydney for Campbelltown-Camden and the money was obviously tempting, but I was struggling with my shoulder injury and that, ultimately, was why I didn't actually go in. We'd agreed a fee and I was on the point of accepting it when I decided I needed to prioritise my rehab.

I wasn't sure how the shoulder would cope with the challenges and frankly, I wasn't all that keen on the idea of living off live insects. I'm sure people would have liked to have seen me eat a cricket or a bug but the diet would have affected my weight and I think there was some concern from the producers that, given my mental health issues, I might struggle.

Actually, I could have handled that side of it. I wouldn't have been the first contestant with mental health issues and cricketers are used to boot camps where you live in tents and get up at 2 am.

The only thing that stopped me was the worry I might jeopardise my rehabilitation. When you're injured you have to treat recovery as a full-time job, so I reluctantly pulled out and instead I watched it on TV like everyone else.

And so I watched a snake sit on Carol Vorderman's face.

I watched Danny Baker narrowly avoid getting sodomised by an eel.

And I pondered the choice between a month in a camp drinking blended camel foreskin and getting maggot facials or a weekend of team bonding in Stoke.

I might be a vegetarian, but I'd take the camel foreskin, every time.

***

My next shot at reality TV stardom was with *Dancing on Ice*, which was basically *Strictly Come Dancing*, but a lot colder. And, as I'd find out, significantly more dangerous.

Dancing on Ice had been off air for four years and I was all set to be part of its big revival. Phillip Schofield and Holly Willoughby were hosting it, Torvill and Dean were the judges and I was set to be the star.

This time everything was agreed, we signed the deal and did all the publicity shots.

Unfortunately I didn't have a lot of experience on ice. No one at the ECB had ever suggested incorporating it into our training regime, although the way I'd celebrated some of my wickets suggested a certain balletic grace that might have come in useful.

The problem was, I suppose, the ice. Not only was it cold, it was hard. Really hard. Geoff Boycott wasn't going to be able to stroll out into the rink and get his keys into this wicket.

I turned up for training in my 'Rocky' gear – a grey, Ralph Lauren jogging suit, and pulled on a pair of giant, black boots that took about half an hour to lace up. We did some training exercises, getting used to gliding on the surface and skating between the kind of plastic cones we used to warm up with at Test matches.

After a while I thought I was getting the hang of it. I ditched the jogging suit for something that looked a bit more Robin Cousins and tried to be more adventurous with a triple turn. The turn was actually beautiful, right up until the moment I tried to come out of it and landed in a heap. I thought I'd landed on a blade or something and suspected my ankle was broken, but my trainer thought it was only twisted.

We went to hospital to get it checked out and by the time we got there I was having a big adrenaline rush, a sure sign that something had gone badly wrong. I couldn't walk on it, let alone skate, and I needed a plate and screws inserted, which, at the time of writing, have only just come out.

I was going to be partnered with a French skater called Melody Le Moal but she ended up skating with the singer Lemar instead. To say I was gutted was an understatement. They did invite me to watch the show, however, and I hobbled along on crutches to do an interview with Phillip Schofield.

My dad wanted me to ask him how he looked so young but, not for the first time in my life, the circuits in my brain tripped and when he put the microphone in front of me I said, 'How come you look thirty-seven, when you're fifty-seven?' As he was only actually fifty-five, I'm not sure he took it as a compliment!

If they still want me back after that I'd love to do it. If I'm selected for the 2020 version, I will attack it!

Chapter 37

Like a Kenwood Chef

Don't be fooled by my calm, collected exterior. When I was on *Celebrity MasterChef*, there were times when I didn't really know what I was doing.

One thing I've learned in life is that when it comes to fine dining, or fine eating, the reason they call it 'fine' is because it just has that extra taste to it, which is why we pay that extra price for it. It's worth it and I think it's quite therapeutic sometimes, once in a while, to enjoy a fine meal with good friends. There's a form of discipline with fine dining, there's etiquette, the way everything is laid out.

So it might come as a surprise to anyone who watched me glide round that kitchen like a Kenwood chef, but I actually know more about eating food than preparing it.

My reality TV debut finally came when my agent, Clive, got me on *MasterChef* in 2018.

If anything, it was even further out of my comfort zone than the jungle or the ice rink. I just couldn't cook at all and in hindsight, it's a miracle I survived my university years. When I got confirmation that I was definitely going on the show I knew I couldn't go in there without some preparation, so my mum gave me a crash course in preparing Indian food and I booked some private tuition so I'd at least have some idea what I was doing.

If you watched the show it might not necessarily have come across that way, but in fact, I actually made quite a lot of progress. In four weeks I went from being just about able to make beans on toast to producing curries, chapatis and raitas, which is a kind of yoghurt.

I didn't know my fellow contestants, but Gregg Wallace and John Torode put us all at ease. They make it a humane show, not like *The Apprentice*, where they seem to make a virtue of cruelty.

I found Gregg in particular very easy to relate to. He understood my sports banter because he loves his rugby and I think one of his personal trainers was a Sikh, so he kind of understood the Sikh culture. The langar, or kitchen, is an essential part of Sikh teachings; there's one in every gurdwara and the idea is that every human is entitled to a meal, no matter who they are, or what their background.

John was more of a cricket man and as he was Australian, I gave him a bit of banter about the Ashes series I'd won against them. He took it pretty well, although being a millionaire with a catering franchise at the SCG probably softened the blow, and we skated over the most recent series, during which they'd beaten us like a lump of dough getting smashed by a rolling pin.

The first challenge was called 'Mystery Box' and we were basically handed some chicken thighs, crabmeat, mascarpone cheese, mango and avocado and told we had fifty minutes to make something with it

OK, chicken. No problem, right? I prepared it, I basted it, I garnished it and I felt cautiously optimistic about it until Gregg came over and asked what I was going to serve with it.

What am I going to *serve* with it?

What am *I* going to serve with it?

What *am* I going to serve with it?

Not again. Not this feeling again. The man standing in front of me was Gregg Wallace, but he might as well have been Peter Moores asking me about my processes. I tried to coax my brain into forming some kind of coherent answer and then I had an idea.

'I'll do it with an omelette!'

Phew. Omelettes are easy! You just have to remember not to burn the egg.

I burned the egg. Not to worry, there's only a nationwide audience of several million people watching.

At this point you may well be wondering how the hell do you burn an egg?

Well, it's not my skill set to be honest. If you want someone to bowl out Sachin Tendulkar, I'm your man. But eggs? That's not really my Luis Boa Morte.

Luckily some of my fellow contestants were in the same boat, especially Gemma Collins, who tried cutting a coconut in half. With a knife.

For the second challenge I was sent to a Latin American restaurant called Coya in Central London, with the actress Chizzy Akudolu and the Paralympian Stef Reid. We were supposed to be cooking over open charcoals and I'll be honest, this could have gone better.

It turns out that if you leave salmon on hot charcoals for too long it turns it black, a lesson most people don't have to learn in front of a television audience in the millions.

When it came to choosing their quarter-finalists, I think Gregg must have felt like Athers did in 1994, when he looked at his fielders and saw Mike Gatting, Martin McCague and Phil Tufnell.

Luckily for me, they liked my cauliflower curry.

In the end they released Chizzy and I was through to the next round, by which time I think I'd improved significantly. The first problem here was that only two out of four of us could go through and my teammate for episode two's first challenge was Stef, a brilliant cook who had one of the places pretty well nailed down.

The second problem was that we were cooking for seventy-five people, at British Airways' training centre in Hounslow.

'These are pilots and cabin crew, so it's really important that they get a square meal,' they told us. The subtext being: feed them, or a 747 might end up dropping out of the sky.

Right. No pressure then.

Having never cooked for more than five people (my immediate family and my dog, Rambo), the scale of it threw me. Admittedly it seemed to throw Gemma more. She was walking round going, 'Should I be worried abaaaht summing?' and asking the head chef, Frank, if he could give her the machine that magically peeled potatoes.

If John and Gregg were like benevolent deputy headmasters, Frank was more like Nasser Hussain when he was delivering one of his bollockings: 'Do you want me to give you a smaller spoon so you can take longer doing it?'

It wasn't the first time I'd been yelled at but it was the first time I'd been yelled at in the kitchen, and I was struggling a bit.

At one point, when I realised we needed to put some rice on, Stef gave me a look. It wasn't angry, just slightly disbelieving, and a bit like Shaun Udal's stunned halibut. I've been getting that look my whole life. In that moment, Stef could have been one of my parents, my teachers, Graham Dilley, Nick Cook, Duncan Fletcher, Michael Vaughan or Mark Robinson.

But we coped. It was physically and mentally as exhausting as a day in the field when Graeme Smith was breaking you slowly, but we got through it and Gregg said the vegetarian curry was 'moreish and addictive'. There was one task left, back at the *MasterChef* kitchen. I knew that for this I was going to have to do something more than bowl a stock delivery.

My speciality was a vegetable biryani. My dad told me it was great, although he'd say that even if I burned it. It was left to Mum to deliver the truth. When I burned the curry, she'd tell me about it all right.

It was still my best option, so I went with the biryani, lentils and chutney.

Clive told me that Gregg loved his desserts so I should probably have made a jam roly-poly, but I gambled and went with what was at least supposed to be a chocolate mousse with cherry kirsch. It actually came out more like a brilliant truffle. I'd tried to bowl a doosra and it had come out as a slider, but what does it matter if it gets the batsman out? Genius often takes unexpected forms.

Gregg said my daal was beautiful and my chutney 'ferocious', but it wasn't quite enough.

We went through for the verdict and it was like waiting for the umpire to put his finger up, although it took what seemed like a few hours instead of what was probably only a few seconds. (Any cricketer who's played in a game Steve Bucknor was umpiring will know how this feels.)

Zoe Lyons was selected alongside Stef, and Gemma and I were out. I was gutted, but I couldn't have done any more and I'd accelerated my processes so much during those few weeks.

I also made an unlikely friend in Gemma, who is, in fact, one of the reasons you're reading this book. I was a little bit unsure about writing it but when I went to see her she said, 'Mont, just go for it.' She's the queen of reality TV and she puts on this facade, but she's really intelligent. After all, she used to sell BMWs in Essex, and that's like being a funeral director in Eastbourne: you're never going to starve in that line of work.

We met up for lunch and I was just so impressed by how shrewd she was. She's written two books, runs her own fashion label and juggles all this with her TV work. Whenever I met her she was almost always on the phone and I was just so impressed with how she managed it all.

When they asked me about her in the Hornchurch dressing room I said I was amazed at how entrepreneurial she was in real life.

They just said, 'Mont, Essex is a county full of business people, it's just the way we are.'

Maybe it's the air.

Chapter 38

Mastermind

I wanted to win *Celebrity Mastermind*. Just as I'd wanted to be famous for my cricketing excellence, I'd wanted to steal the show by racking up an unassailable lead in my specialist subject and then picking off the general knowledge questions, like Jonty Rhodes snaring catches at backward point.

It didn't quite happen like that. It wasn't the first time in my life that people had suggested I was on another planet and I think perhaps I was … one that was orbiting 10 per cent slower than Earth.

We were on a really tight schedule, which didn't help. Early that morning Clive and I met at Euston. I was able to revise on the train, but as soon as we got to Manchester a car was waiting and we were taken straight to the studio.

There was barely any time to think before I was actually sitting in the chair. I thought the first round went OK, but I'd had a plan that had backfired because I didn't realise you had to wait for the whole question to be read out. I interrupted John Humphrys and then had to get him to repeat a question. It probably only cost me a handful of seconds although it seemed a lot longer.

I wasn't aware at the time that Humphrys had a reputation for interrupting his interviewees. In hindsight I can see the irony in failing to let him finish his question, but at the time I didn't think a lot of it.

I got six out of eight and thought I'd done pretty well, but back in the dressing room I can remember asking everyone their scores and no one really wanted to talk about them.

'I got nine,' one said, reluctantly.

'Eight,' said another.

'Ten,' said the third.

Ah. So maybe I hadn't done as well as I thought I had. A chink of doubt crept in as I thought maybe I'm not going to win this after all. That chink widened when I sat back in the soft, leathery chair and looked at John Humprhys' soft, leathery face.

'I don't really know anything about cricket,' he said, and my confidence took another knock. When I looked at him it was like I was looking at Prince Philip. He had a real presence of royalty about him. We made awkward conversation for a few seconds and then he bowled me a long hop for the opening question.

'How many pockets are there on a snooker table?'

Almost too easy. 'Six!' I said. *I'm on my way.*

'What sign of the zodiac is represented by a crab?'

'Scorpion ... Sagittarius?'

'Cancer.' *Shit. I knew that.*

'What is the title of A.A. Milne's stage adaptation of Kenneth Graham's *The Wind in the Willows*?'

Fuck. No Idea. We're back in Dhoni territory now. If I hold my hands out there's a chance, however small, that I might just catch him. If I don't hold my hands out ...

'Harry Potter?'

'Toad of Toad Hall.' *Never mind, if it comes to a tiebreaker it'll be decided on passes, so it's better to give the wrong answer than no answer.*

'Henry VIII had six wives, three called Catherine, two called Anne and one who died shortly after giving birth. What was her name?'

No idea. Think of something vaguely royal.

'Elizabeth?'

'Jane. What is the standard international unit of absolute temperature? It is indicated by the letter K.'

'Oh, gosh ... pass.'

'Which Asian island city state is served by Changi International Airport?'

Wherever it is I haven't heard of it, but it sounds a bit like ...

'Shanghai?'

'Singapore.' *Fuck's sake!*

'Birds described as pelagic describe most of their lives flying over what?'

'The sky?' *How do you fly over the sky?*

'In what '97 film do a group of unemployed men become strippers for the night in their local working men's club?'

I've had it now. My head's gone. 'The Dreamboys?'

'The Full Monty.' *Oh fuck me ...*

'In which city is the Olympiastadion, built for the 1972 Olympics and where Germany's national football team played matches until 2001?'

'Er ... Athens?'

'Munich.'

By now I know. I can already imagine the eruption on Twitter. I just want this all to end, but in the parallel universe I inhabit, sixty seconds seems like a decade.

'What was the second volume of C.S. Lewis's *Chronicles of Narnia* to be published, following on from *The Magician's Nephew?*'

I'm in a private hell, where I'm playing cricket, but I'm stuck in the field, unable to bowl, chasing every single delivery to the boundary and never quite getting there in time.

What's Narnia and why does it merit seven chronicles? I'm giving up now. I'm lobbing this one in underarm. 'C.J. Lewis?'

'The Lion, The Witch and The Wardrobe.'

Oh right. That *one.*

'Kimberlite, an igneous rock named after the South African city of Kimberley, is a source of what very precious stones?'

I'm smiling now. Smiling like Del Boy when he realises Raquel is a stripper. 'Dunno. Pass.'

'What were the five guys in the title of the hit musical that was a tribute to the jazz bluesman Louis Jordan?'

Literally never heard of him. 'Pass.'

'In an 1819 poem ...'

This is going to end well ...

'what season of the year does Keats ...

Who?

'describe as a season of mists and mellow fruitfulness?'

I wasn't listening. No point asking him to repeat it. 1819, what would have been written around 1819 ...?

'Oliver Twist?'

'Autumn!'

Oh fuck. Humphrys laughs. He actually laughs. Just make it stop.

'In which city is the television series *Cheers* set?'

My brain is capsizing and as it slowly dawns on me that I've answered Oliver Twist *to a question about the four seasons, I realise that I haven't been listening to this one. Where was* Cheers *set?*

'America.'

'Boston.'

Half a point for getting the right continent?

'What national survey has been held in Britain every ten years since 1801, except 1941 because of the Second World War?'

The beeps sound. It'll soon be over. 'I'll give it to you, shall I?' says John. 'It was the census.'

'OK.'

Car crash doesn't really do it justice. It was like the *Titanic* ramming the *Hindenburg*, and before anyone points out that a boat can't ram an airship, remember that by this point I was on my planet, where my rules apply.

In the moments immediately afterwards I was angry, because it was so embarrassing. Clive was chuckling to himself and yet when we went over the questions afterwards I got most of them right. I think the *Mastermind* seat got to me.

When it went out I was with my family and I didn't want to watch it, but for me to say *Oliver Twist* was, I suppose, why there's only one Monty Panesar. I think it's just my character and my personality and it's why people remember me. Hundreds of professional cricketers drop catches every year, but not many of them drop them with the élan I managed to display when dropping Dhoni.

Hardly anyone will remember who won that episode of *Celebrity Mastermind*. They'll remember me all right.

A couple of weeks later I watched *Dancing on Ice* and saw Gemma Collins fall flat on her face. My first thought was 'I hope she's all right', and when I realised she was OK and watched it again, I just couldn't stop laughing. It was like when a cricketer gets hit in the box and his teammates don't know whether to ask if he's OK or collapse with the giggles.

Gemma just got back up again as if nothing had happened. In life, it's not how we fall that matters; it's how we rise again.

Epilogue

Monty Panesar 2.0

I'm not giving up cricket yet. I enjoy it too much and I think that for my physical and mental well-being I should carry on playing for as long as I can, whether it's first class cricket or club cricket on a village green.

Realistically, however, I'm not likely to be taking that many five-wicket hauls for England. I'm running out of time if I want to conjure that ball of the millennium and as things stand, I'm 633 wickets short of Murali's record. I did, however, get to meet both Henry Blofeld and Prince Philip and I'm still up for the knighthood if he is.

It's time for the second part of my life to start. I don't know exactly what I'm going to do, but whatever I do next, I want to do something that gives me the same level of success, because I don't want to be remembered, when I'm forty-five or fifty, as someone who just played cricket for England.

It may be politics, or the entertainment industry. I could become a public figure and maybe a TV personality. I'd like people to come up to me and say, 'How's your chat show going?' or, 'I love your new game show'. I would love to be an actor in Bollywood, or preferably Hollywood. You've got to think so big, or you're not going to get there in life.

One thing I'd really like to do is have my own series, like Freddie has with *A League of Their Own*, and I've already launched my own YouTube channel, which you should definitely subscribe to if you haven't already.

Above all, I'd like to inspire people. I'm a British Asian boy from Luton who played for England, broke down social barriers and hopefully blazed a trail for Sikh sportsmen and women all over the UK.

Beyond that, if you have ever suffered with mental health issues, I hope this story helps you to rebuild your life. You may experience moments, like I did, when everyone seems to be out to get you, but you'll find they aren't. When you're at your lowest you'll realise that people have an overwhelming desire to help you. Don't be afraid to ask them.

I was low for a while, but with the help of people who cared, I put my issues behind me and I'm now determined to enjoy the rest of my life.

I think I passed the cricket test. Now it's time to see what happens next.

Afterword

by

Fred Atkins

The final interview for this book took place in a Central London restaurant called Park Chinois.

We'd met outside Green Park Tube station and Monty was in the mood for a Chinese.

'I tell you what, mate, we are going to have a fucking nice meal,' he said. He wasn't wrong.

By now I was getting used to Monty. He'd travel down from Luton, I'd come up from Maidstone and we'd meet in the same spot, usually half an hour after the agreed time.

I'd been warned about his punctuality, both by his agent Clive Hart, who'd said, 'I can't stress how important it is that you text him the day beforehand to remind him,' and through reading the autobiography he'd written in 2007 with Richard Hobson.

In the end, although he was habitually late, he always texted ahead to apologise. When he did turn up he usually wanted to go the Ritz, a plan I always torpedoed by wearing trainers because I was worried we'd blow our expenses budget in a single sitting.

For me a Chinese meant a £24 takeaway from the Lotus House on the Tonbridge Road. For Monty it was an £80 per head meal in a Mayfair restaurant decorated like an imperial palace.

'Hey, I'm from London, we're more sophisticated than you are down in Kent.'

'You're from Luton!'

'It's close.'

I think he was joking, although it wasn't easy to tell. I was beginning to understand why batsmen found him so difficult to read.

I checked when I got home. I lived 7 miles further out.

After I'd asked the last of my questions we both had half an hour to kill before our next appointments, so I asked Monty who he thought would be the cricketer most likely to keep him sane if he were ever stranded on a desert island.

He didn't answer, though by now I'd learned this was just his natural thinking time. After what seemed like five minutes and was probably only a few seconds, he said, 'Can I pick a few? I'd definitely have Michael Vaughan there. I think Andrew Strauss is a good one. Andrew Flintoff, Virender Sehwag, he's the funniest. Shahid Afridi, Andrew Symonds, Harbhajan Singh, Zaheer Khan, Shoaib Akhtar …'

I tried interrupting him to say this desert island was about to get crowded, but he just carried on.

'Can I have Graeme Swann?'

'I guess so.'

'What about Mike Hussey? Actually I found Graeme Smith a really nice guy away from cricket. I never really got to know him. I think I'd like to have Wasim Akram there …'

This was classic Monty. When he was in the mood you couldn't stop him.

I'd first met him outside a hospitality marquee in Weston-super-Mare, where he was playing for Lashings and posing, obligingly, for a selfie, with a group of forty-something women.

I was there in my day job as Lashings' media manager. Clive Hart had said he was interested in writing a second autobiography and said I should ask him about it during the Weston match. We subsequently started a conversation that was interrupted approximately every thirty seconds.

We'd barely introduced ourselves before we heard a cry of: 'Monty! It's no good, your eyes were shut, we're going to have to do it again!'

A fleeting expression of panic crossed Monty's face, but it passed. He smiled, restaged the photo, kept his eyes open this time and everyone went away happy.

It was obvious to everyone at the game that Monty was the stellar attraction. There were other bowlers there with more first class wickets and several batsmen with many more first class runs, but the selfie that everyone wanted was with Monty.

Kids too young to have seen him bowl in anger loved Monty. Middle-aged housewives with no interest in cricket loved Monty. Everyone seemed to love Monty and the feeling appeared to be mutual.

Monty Panesar is in a good place now, but he hasn't always been this contented. There's a dark side to the gentlemen's game and there always has been. A century before Monty Panesar became England's leading spin bowler, his predecessor Colin Blythe suffered from a debilitating 'mystery' ailment that sometimes left him physically unable to bowl.

The doomed Blythe, killed by a German shell near Ypres in 1917, was once euphemistically described as 'exhausted' after taking fifteen wickets in a Test match in 1907. In reality, Blythe was an epileptic and a century after his death, cricket writers were still speculating that his condition was worsened by the stresses of playing Test match cricket.

By 2019, these stresses are well known, but still not widely understood. In the time since Monty made his Test debut in 2006, an astonishing number of cricketers have seen their careers damaged, and in some cases ended, by mental health issues.

Trescothick, Flintoff, Harmison, Yardy, Trott, Gilchrist … Panesar.

This isn't a problem exclusive to cricket. The Weston match took place the day after the 2018 Champions League final between Real Madrid and Liverpool, a match defined by two horrendous goalkeeping errors by a possibly concussed Loris Karius. Every time a fielder dropped a catch or let a ball run past him, someone on the boundary cracked a joke about it being an audition for the Liverpool job.

Monty, by now commentating, smiled along, but he didn't join in with the ridicule. He'd worn that hat before, when his fielding became notorious at the start of his England career. Before Monty it was Kevin Pietersen, after Monty it was Steven Finn. As a professional sportsman who knew what it was like to be the scapegoat, he wanted to talk about Gareth Bale's wonder goal instead.

'We should be celebrating one of the greatest goals of all time,' he told the crowd. 'Gareth Bale comes from a country that is part of Great Britain and we should be patriotic about it.'

For someone who freely confesses to being shy, Monty was a natural in the commentary box. He talked persuasively about the disproportionately low numbers of British Asian cricketers who make it from club level through to the professional ranks. He commentated naturally on his teammates, bantering with them easily but never with an edge. Their affection for him was obvious and genuine.

He was at ease, now, but in the previous five years he'd been accused of urinating on a nightclub bouncer; of refusing to bowl or field when asked; of alcohol abuse; and of being so paranoid his county had to effectively suspend him.

As a result, there was significant interest in his side of the story, but some of the publishers wanted a misery memoir.

I didn't think that was the best approach and neither did he. When I thought of Monty I thought of a line Alex Ferguson once wrote in the foreword to Barry Fry's autobiography: 'It was impossible to think of him without smiling. He's a naturally funny man with a gift for making people laugh, intentionally or otherwise.' When we finally got to talk properly, we agreed. The story needed to be told with humour and humanity.

Our second meeting was at Lashings' next match, at Odiham in Hampshire. 'Hi Fred, how you doing?' he said, and I felt secretly pleased that he'd remembered my name.

He didn't always remember it. He kept calling me Frank and he once asked, 'What's your name?' even after we'd had several meetings.

I didn't take it personally and besides, I was in good company. At one point during the final interview he said Andy Flower was one of the elite coaches in English sport, alongside Clive Woodward and 'Sir Alex Beresford', who I deduced had to be a hybrid of Dave Brailsford and Alex Ferguson.

Together we wanted to write a feel-good book. I hope we've succeeded. And as he said to me as he ordered a £16 ice cream and I tried to calculate if we'd blown the entertainment budget in one sitting: 'If nothing else happens, we'll always have had this meal.'

About the Author

Fred Atkins is a freelance journalist and author who covered the England cricket team for the Associated Press from 2009 to 2013 and now works for the Lashings World XI cricket team.

After graduating from Sussex University he spent three years teaching English in Greece and fell into journalism when he landed a job as sports reporter for the Maidstone News. He became sports editor of the Kent Messenger and covered the 2007 Tour de France before going freelance.

His previous books include "Arsenal: The French Connection" (2012), Exodus: Maidstone United 1988-2012 (2016) and a novel called "Welcome to Kent: Sorry About The Racists" (2017), the story of a floundering local newspaper that subsists on stories about custard powder shortages, killer potholes and newsagents that sell out of date pasties until it becomes embroiled in an email hacking scandal.

He is married with a daughter.

Fred would like to thank: Dave Fitzgerald of Lashings for the recommendation, Richard Sydenham for his advice, Clive Hart for making it happen and, of course, Monty Panesar.

Monty Panesar Career Statistics

Compiled by Ian Marshall

Mudhsuden Singh 'Monty' Panesar, born Luton, Bedfordshire, 25 April 1982

Left-hand bat; slow left-arm bowler

Wisden Cricketer of the Year 2006

Northamptonshire 2001-16; cap 2006

Sussex 2010-13; cap 2010

Essex 2013-15

Loughborough UCCE 2004

Lions 2009-10

TEST MATCH CAREER RECORD

Bowling	Tests	O	M	Runs	Wkts	Avge	Best	5wI	10wM
2005-06 to 2013-14	50	2079.1	468	5797	167	34.71	6-37	12	2

Match list

Opponent	Venue	Date	1st Inns	2nd Inns	Res
1. v India	Nagpur	1-5 Mar 2006	2-73	1-58	Drawn
2. v India	Mohali	9-13 Mar 2006	1-65	0-48	Lost
3. v India	Mumbai	18-22 Mar 2006	1-53	0-15	Won
4. v Sri Lanka	Lord's	11-15 May 2006	DNB	2-49	Drawn
5. v Sri Lanka	Birmingham	25-28 May 2006	1-7	2-73	Won
6. v Sri Lanka	Nottingham	2-5 Jun 2006	0-3	5-78	Lost
7. v Pakistan	Lord's	13-17 Jul 2006	0-93	2-60	Drawn
8. v Pakistan	Manchester	27-29 Jul 2006	3-21	5-72	Won
9. v Pakistan	Leeds	4-8 Aug 2006	3-127	3-39	Won
10. v Pakistan	The Oval	17-20 Aug 2006	1-103	–	Won*
11. v Australia	Perth	14-18 Dec 2006	5-92	3-145	Lost

Opponent	Venue	Date	1st Inns	2nd Inns	Res
12. v Australia	Melbourne	26-28 Dec 2006	0-52	-	Lost
13. v Australia	Sydney	2-5 Jan 2007	2-90	DNB	Lost
14. v West Indies	Lord's	17-21 May 2007	6-129	0-13	Drawn
15. v West Indies	Leeds	25-28 May 2007	0-1	1-20	Won
16. v West Indies	Manchester	7-11 Jun 2007	4-50	6-137	Won
17. v West Indies	Chester-le-St	15-19 Jun 2007	1-34	5-46	Won
18. v India	Lord's	19-23 Jul 2007	0-22	2-63	Drawn
19. v India	Nottingham	27-31 Jul 2007	4-101	DNB	Lost
20. v India	The Oval	9-13 Aug 2007	2-159	0-58	Drawn
21. v Sri Lanka	Kandy	1-5 Dec 2007	3-46	3-132	Lost
22. v Sri Lanka	Colombo, SSC	9-13 Dec 2007	2-151	-	Drawn
23. v Sri Lanka	Galle	18-22 Dec 2007	0-76	-	Drawn
24. v New Zealand	Hamilton	5-9 Mar 2008	1-101	3-50	Lost
25. v New Zealand	Wellington	13-17 Mar 2008	0-2	1-53	Won
26. v New Zealand	Napier	22-26 Mar 2008	0-0	6-126	Won
27. v New Zealand	Lord's	15-19 May 2008	1-30	1-56	Drawn
28. v New Zealand	Manchester	23-26 May 2008	1-101	6-37	Won
29. v New Zealand	Nottingham	5-8 Jun 2008	DNB	0-21	Won
30. v South Africa	Lord's	10-14 Jul 2008	4-74	0-116	Drawn
31. v South Africa	Leeds	18-21 Jul 2008	3-65	DNB	Lost
32. v South Africa	Birmingham	30 Jul-2 Aug 2008	0-25	2-91	Lost
33. v South Africa	The Oval	7-11 Aug 2008	2-4	2-37	Won
34. v India	Chennai	11-15 Dec 2008	3-65	0-105	Lost
35. v India	Mohali	19-23 Dec 2008	2-89	1-44	Drawn
36. v West Indies	Kingston	4-7 Feb 2009	1-122	-	Lost
37. v West Indies	North Sound	13 Feb 2009	-	-	Drawn
38. v West Indies	Port of Spain	6-10 Mar 2009	2-114	2-34	Drawn
39. v Australia	Cardiff	8-12 Jul 2009	1-115	-	Drawn
40. v Pakistan	Abu Dhabi	25-28 Jan 2012	1-91	6- 62	Lost
41. v Pakistan	Dubai, DSC	3-6 Feb 2012	2-25	5-124	Lost
42. v Sri Lanka	Galle	26-29 Mar 2012	0-42	2-59	Lost
43. v India	Mumbai	23-26 Nov 2012	5-129	6-81	Won
44. v India	Kolkata	5-9 Dec 2012	4-90	1-75	Won
45. v India	Nagpur	13-17 Dec 2012	1-81	-	Drawn
46. v New Zealand	Dunedin	6-10 Mar 2013	1-83	-	Drawn
47. v New Zealand	Wellington	14-18 Mar 2013	0-47	1-44	Drawn
48. v New Zealand	Auckland	22-26 Mar 2013	1-123	2-53	Drawn
49. v Australia	Adelaide	5-9 Dec 2013	1-157	1-41	Lost
50. v Australia	Melbourne	26-29 Dec 2013	0-18	1-41	Lost

* Match awarded to England after Pakistan refused to play. DNB = Did not bowl in an innings;
- = England did not bowl in this innings

England's Top 10 Spin-Bowling Wicket-Takers †

	Tests	Wkts	Avge	Best	5wI	10wM
D.L. Underwood	86	297	25.83	8-51	17	6
G.P. Swann	60	255	29.96	6-65	17	3
J.C. Laker	46	193	21.24	10-53	9	3
M.M. Ali	58	177	36.37	6-53	5	1
G.A.R. Lock	49	174	25.58	7-35	9	3
M.S. Panesar	**50**	**167**	**34.71**	**6-37**	**12**	**2**
F.J. Titmus	53	153	32.22	7-79	7	–
J.E. Emburey	64	147	38.40	7-78	6	–
H. Verity	40	144	24.37	8-43	5	2
A.F. Giles	54	143	40.60	5-57	5	–

Most Five-Wicket Hauls by England Bowlers †

	Tests	Wkts	5wI
I.T. Botham	102	383	27
J.M. Anderson	148	575	27
S.F. Barnes	27	189	24
G.P. Swann	60	255	17
F.S. Trueman	67	307	17
D.L. Underwood	86	297	17
R.G.D. Willis	90	325	16
S.C.J. Broad	126	437	16
A.V. Bedser	51	236	15
A.R.C. Fraser	46	177	13
A.R. Caddick	62	234	13
M.S. Panesar	**50**	**167**	**12**

† Figures correct to 1 July 2019.

Most Frequent Victims

B.B. McCullum	New Zealand	6	J.M. How	New Zealand	3
L.R.P.L. Taylor	New Zealand	5	Inzaman-ul-Haq	Pakistan	3
A.B. de Villiers	South Africa	4	Mohammad Hafeez	Pakistan	3
M.S. Dhoni	India	4	Mohammad Yousuf	Pakistan	3
S.L. Malinga	Sri Lanka	4	Z. Khan	India	3
D.S. Smith	West Indies	4	M. Morkel	South Africa	3
S.R. Tendulkar	India	4	R.S. Morton	West Indies	3
Asad Shafiq	Pakistan	3	D. Ramdin	West Indies	3
C.D. Collymore	West Indies	3	A. Symonds	Australia	3
Faisal Iqbal	Pakistan	3	Younis Khan	Pakistan	3

Batting	Tests	I	NO	HS	Runs	Avge	50	100	Ct
2005-06 to 2013-14	50	68	23	26	220	4.88	–	–	10

His top score in Test matches was 26 v Sri Lanka at Nottingham on 2-5 June 2006.

LIMITED-OVERS INTERNATIONAL CAREER RECORD

Bowling	LOI	O	M	Runs	Wkts	Avge	Best	4w	R/R
2006-07 to 2007-08	26	218	10	980	24	40.83	3-25	–	4.49

Match list

Opponent	Venue	Date	Figs	Result
1. v Australia	Melbourne	12 Jan 2007	1-46	Lost
2. v New Zealand	Hobart	16 Jan 2007	1-36	Won
3. v New Zealand	Adelaide	23 Jan 2007	1-44	Lost
4. v Australia	Adelaide	26 Jan 2007	0-19	Lost
5. v New Zealand	Perth	30 Jan 2007	2-35	Lost
6. v Australia	Sydney	2 Feb 2007	1-64	Won
7. v New Zealand	Brisbane	6 Feb 2007	1-38	Won
8. v Australia	Melbourne	9 Feb 2007	2-44	Won
9. v Australia	Sydney	11 Feb 2007	0-15	Won
10. v New Zealand	Gros Islet	16 Mar 2007	1-47	Lost
11. v Canada	Gros Islet	18 Mar 2007	1-35	Won
12. v Kenya	Gros Islet	24 Mar 2007	0-28	Won
13. v Ireland	Providence	30 Mar 2007	2-31	Won
14. v Sri Lanka	North Sound	4 Apr 2007	0-45	Lost
15. v Australia	North Sound	8 Apr 2007	0-48	Lost
16. v Bangladesh	Bridgetown	11 Apr 2007	3-25	Won
17. v South Africa	Bridgetown	17 Apr 2007	0-24	Lost
18. v West Indies	Lord's	1 Jul 2007	1-29	Won
19. v West Indies	Nottingham	7 Jul 2007	0-28	Lost
20. v India	Southampton	21 Aug 2007	1-47	Won
21. v India	Birmingham	27 Aug 2007	1-49	Won
22. v India	Manchester	30 Aug 2007	1-39	Won
23. v India	Leeds	2 Sep 2007	1-50	Lost
24. v India	The Oval	5 Sep 2007	1-55	Lost
25. v India	Lord's	8 Sep 2007	1-28	Won
26. v Sri Lanka	Colombo, RPS	13 Oct 2007	1-31	Lost

Batting	LOI	I	NO	HS	Runs	Avge	50	100	Ct
2006-07 to 2007-08	26	8	3	13	26	5.20	–	–	3

His top score in limited-overs internationals was 13 v West Indies at Nottingham on 7 July 2007.

FIRST CLASS CAREER RECORD

Debut, Northamptonshire v Leicestershire at Northampton on 23-26 August 2001, taking 4-120 and 4-11. N.D. Burns was his maiden wicket.

Final game, Northamptonshire v Worcestershire at Northampton on 10-12 July 2016, taking 0-35 and 1-75. E.G. Barnard was his final wicket.

In 2006, he was the third highest wicket-taker in the country, behind Mushtaq Ahmed (101) and Z. Khan (78); in 2011, he was the sixth highest.

	P	O	M	Runs	Wkts	Ave	Best	5wI	10wM
Northamptonshire 2001	2	101.3	28	358	11	32.54	4-11	-	-
Br Unis/Northants 2002	6	190.5	55	554	17	32.58	4-42	-	-
ECB Acad in SL 2002-03	2	74.3	27	209	10	20.90	5-77	1	-
Northamptonshire 2003	6	161.2	30	557	13	42.84	3-92	-	-
Loughboro UCCE 2004	3	86.0	23	197	5	39.40	3-28	-	-
Br Unis/Northants 2005	9	429.2	106	1146	51	22.47	7-181	4	1
England in India 2005-06	4	142.0	38	378	7	54.00	2-73	-	-
Nhants/MCC/England 2006	17	759.0	195	2029	71	28.57	5-32	6	1
England in Aus 2006-07	4	124.3	19	467	12	38.91	5-92	1	-
Northants/England 2007	12	464.1	88	1413	53	26.66	6-65	4	1
England in S Lanka 2007-08	4	166.0	27	486	11	44.18	3-46	-	-
Eng Lions in India 2007-08	2	58.0	10	194	5	38.80	3-106	-	-
Eng in N Zealand 2007-08	4	133.5	33	359	13	27.61	6-126	1	-
Northants/England 2008	14	530.5	98	1525	40	38,12	6-37	2	-
England in India 2008-09	2	79.0	10	303	6	50.50	3-65	-	-
England in WI 2008-09	3	109.5	29	270	5	54.00	2-34	-	-
Northants/England 2009	15	454.5	97	1195	22	54.31	3-10	-	-
Lions (S Africa) 2009-10	6	210.4	43	586	15	39.06	4-42	-	-
Sussex/Eng Lions 2010	16	518.2	135	1336	52	25.69	5-44	2	-
England in Aus 2010-11	2	84.0	12	247	6	41.16	3-63	-	-
Sussex 2011	16	750.3	223	1880	69	27.24	5-58	3	-
Eng in UAE v Pak 2011-12	3	184.3	59	405	22	18.40	6-62	3	-
England in S Lanka 2011-12	2	88.3	36	170	8	21.25	5-37	1	-
Sussex 2012	16	514.1	157	1227	53	23.15	7-60	2	1
England in India 2012-13	4	221.0	57	526	19	27.68	6-81	2	1
Eng in N Zealand 2012-13	3	130.2	46	350	5	70.00	2-53	-	-
Sussex/Essex 2013	18	558.0	131	1543	40	38.57	5-95	2	-
England in Aus 2013-14	2	70.5	9	257	3	85.66	1-41	-	-
MCC in UAE 2013-14	1	45.2	6	129	7	18.42	5-63	1	-
Essex 2014	15	403.2	114	1144	46	24.86	6-111	4	1
Essex 2015	3	75.1	17	270	7	38.57	4-112	-	-
Northamptonshire 2016	3	112.0	16	425	5	85.00	3-122	-	-

	P	O	M	Runs	Wkts	Ave	Best	5wI	10wM
Northamptonshire	58	2255.5	508	6522	191	34.14	7-181	10	2
Sussex	59	2149.2	596	5474	200	27.37	7-60	9	1
Essex	24	668.1	181	1918	67	28.62	6-111	4	1
Lions	6	210.4	43	586	15	39.06	4-42	-	-
England †	60	2395.1	558	6558	201	32.62	6-37	14	2
ECB Academy	2	74.3	27	209	10	20.90	5-77	1	-
England Lions	3	60.0	10	202	5	40.40	3-106	-	-
Loughborough UCCE	3	86.0	23	197	5	39.40	3-28	-	-
British Universities	2	56.1	16	207	7	29.57	3-48	-	-
MCC	2	76.2	12	262	8	32.75	5-63	1	-
Total	219	8032.1	1974	22135	709	31.22	7-60	39	6

† *Total includes ten tour matches that were not Tests.*

Six or More Wickets in an Innings

Match	Venue	Date	Figures
Northamptonshire v Essex	Chelmsford	10–12 July 2005	56.3-15-181-7
Northamptonshire v Worcs	Northampton	20–23 July 2005	26.5-3-77-6
England v West Indies	Lord's	17–21 May 2007	36.1-3-129-6
England v West Indies	Manchester	7–11 June 2007	51.5-13-137-6
Northamptonshire v Glos	Northampton	8–11 July 2007	28-7-65-6
England v New Zealand	Napier	22–26 March 2008	46-17-126-6
England v New Zealand	Manchester	23–26 May 2008	17-5-37-6
England v Pakistan	Abu Dhabi	25–28 January 2012	38.2-18-62-6
Sussex v Somerset	Taunton	21–24 August 2012	31.5-8-60-7
Sussex v Somerset	Taunton	21–24 August 2012	26.5-6-77-6
England v India	Mumbai	23–26 November 2012	22-3-81-6
Essex v Leicestershire	Chelmsford	4–7 May 2014	50-19-111-6
Essex v Glamorgan	Swansea	15–18 August 2014	45-15-118-6

Batting	Matches	I	NO	HS	Runs	Avge	50	100	Ct
2001 to 2016	219	270	87	46*	1536	8.39	-	-	44

His highest score of 46* (104 balls, 116 mins, 5 fours) was made for Sussex v Middlesex at Hove on 5-8 May 2010.

LIST-A CAREER RECORD

Debut, Northamptonshire v Essex at Colchester on 25 August 2002, scoring 16* and taking 0-26.

Final game, Essex v Sri Lankans at Chelmsford on 13 May 2014, taking 2-27, did not bat.

	P	O	M	Runs	Wkts	Ave	Best	4wI	R/R
Northamptonshire 2002	1	9.0	0	26	0	-	-	-	2.88
ECB Acad in SL 2002-03	2	14.0	3	46	5	9.20	5-20	1	3.28
Northamptonshire 2003	1	6.0	0	36	1	36.00	1-36	-	6.00
Northamptonshire 2005	1	9.0	1	30	0	-	-	-	3.33
Northamptonshire 2006	6	43.0	0	199	5	39.80	2-24	-	4.62
England in Aus 2006-07	9	74.0	4	341	9	37.88	2-35	-	4.60
England in WI 2006-07	8	64.0	4	283	7	40.42	3-25	-	4.42
Nhants/England 2007	9	78.0	2	357	9	39.66	2-32	-	4.57
England in SL 2007-08	1	10.0	0	31	1	31.00	1-31	-	3.10
Northamptonshire 2008	6	41.0	2	169	6	28.16	3-36	-	4.12
Northamptonshire 2009	10	58.1	1	302	8	37.75	2-27	-	5.19
Sussex 2010	12	85.4	4	406	14	29.00	3-21	-	4.73
Sussex 2011	13	91.0	2	474	13	36.46	2-28	-	5.20
Sussex 2012	5	34.0	0	165	3	55.00	1-29	-	4.85
Essex 2014	1	4.0	0	27	2	13.50	2-27	-	6.75
Northamptonshire	26	174.1	4	794	22	36.09	3-36	-	4.55
Sussex	30	210.4	6	1045	30	34.83	3-21	-	4.96
Essex	1	4.0	0	27	2	13.50	2-27	-	6.75
England	26	218.0	10	980	24	40.83	3-25	-	4.49
ECB Nat Academy	2	14.0	3	46	5	9.20	5-20	1	3.28
Total	**85**	**620.5**	**23**	**2892**	**83**	**34.84**	**5-20**	**1**	**4.65**

His best figures of 5-20 came for the ECB National Academy v Sri Lanka A at Nondescripts CC, Colombo, on 19 March 2003.

Batting	Matches	I	NO	HS	Runs	Avge	50	100	Ct
2002 to 2014	85	29	13	17*	141	8.81	-	-	15

His highest score of 17* (12 balls, 16 mins, 2 fours) was made for Northamptonshire v Leicestershire at Northampton on 10 May 2008.

TWENTY20 CAREER RECORD

Debut, Northamptonshire v Warwickshire at Northampton on 27 June 2006, scoring 2 and taking 0–39.

Final game, Essex v Glamorgan at Chelmsford on 23 May 2014, taking 0–37, did not bat.

	P	O	M	Runs	Wkts	Avge	Best	4wI	R/R
Northamptonshire 2006	6	24.0	0	195	8	24.37	2–22	–	8.12
England in Aus 2006–07	1	4.0	0	40	2	20.00	2–40	–	10.00
Northamptonshire 2008	3	6.0	0	59	1	59.00	1–21	–	9.83
Northamptonshire 2009	9	27.0	0	167	1	167.00	1–22	–	6.18
Sussex 2011	12	42.0	0	297	15	19.80	3–14	–	7.07
Essex 2014	2	5.0	0	58	0	–	–	–	11.60
Total	33	108.0	0	816	27	30.22	3–14	-	7.55

His best figures of 3–14 came for Sussex v Gloucestershire at Bristol on 5 June 2011.

Batting	Matches	I	NO	HS	Runs	Avge	50	100	Ct
2006 to 2014	33	7	2	3*	7	1.40	–	–	3